The Laughing Dingo

The Laughing Dingo

and other neighbours

Bryce Fraser

ALLEN & UNWIN

To Tricia

© Bryce Fraser 1994

Illustrations by Jane Ingham

First published in 1994
Allen & Unwin Pty Ltd
9 Atchison Street, St Leonards, NSW 2065 Australia

National Library of Australia
Cataloguing-in-Publication entry:

Fraser, Bryce.
  The laughing dingo.

  ISBN 1 86373 568 2.
  I. Title.

A823.3

Set in 10/12 pt Palatino by DOCUPRO, Sydney
Printed by Griffin Paperbacks, Adelaide

10 9 8 7 6 5 4 3 2 1

Contents

1

Playing possum

The ceiling of the kitchen had grown a tail. Or so it seemed. A long, black-tipped, furry, grey tail protruded through a ragged hole waving to and fro like a piece of seaweed on the shore of a gentle sea.

Jock Muir glanced up without pausing in his dialogue, ignored it; so did his wife Jean. So I ignored it as though it was an everyday occurrence for a ceiling suddenly to grow a tail. Slowly, the tail slid upwards until it disappeared through the hole. Then a grey 'arm' with a soft paw and long sharp claws appeared.

Sitting in the adjoining dining area, elbows on the table, chin propped comfortably in my hands, I was looking directly into the kitchen. The paw was less easy to ignore than the tail because it waved about in erratic circles and did figure-of-eight patterns, not at all like soothing seaweed, more like a hand searching in the dark for a keyhole at the end of a long night in the pub.

In my relaxed, chin-in-hands, elbows-on-the-table position my head was pretty well immobile, so I found my eyes following the path of the paw, doing circles and figures of eight in much the way I do when practising eye exercises.

Jock's exposition on the refraction of light in crystals ceased abruptly just as my pupils were swooping down to the right-hand corners of my eye sockets. I had only to give the pupils

a bit of a nudge to bring his sharp features into focus. He was looking at me inquiringly over the top of his glasses.

'Go away, Nibbles,' said Jean, who was sitting opposite me with her back to the kitchen. 'We're talking.' Even though she couldn't see it, she was well aware that their resident brushtail possum was the cause of the distraction. After all, she spent much of her time in the kitchen with the tail dangling above her like a forgotten Christmas decoration.

But Jock put down his cigarette, got up, went to the nearby refrigerator, took out a lettuce leaf, held it up and brushed it against the paw that immediately formed a fist, clutching it. Paw and lettuce disappeared through the hole that no doubt had been gouged by the enterprising Nibbles knowing that a straight line was the shortest distance between his bedroom and the refrigerator. The soft, cane-fibre ceiling sagged hammock-like under the weight of possums that had been using it as a pad for years.

Jock looked out through the wide, glass-panelled front doors at the last glow of the sun on the ridge across the harbour. 'It's time for him to get up. He'll call by before long.'

There was a scrabbling sound above us and I visualised the nocturnal Nibbles extricating himself, squeezing between the ceiling and galvanised iron sheeting, then somehow doing a 180-degree turn the way possums can to get on to the roof.

Jock was now slicing up an apple and I noticed that, as usual, he was bulging. This is not to imply that he was a fat man: on the contrary he was slight, somewhat less than average height and lean and wiry. The bulges were in his pockets. I'm sure that Jock chose his clothes, not for their sartorial qualities, but for the number and size of the pockets. I hadn't thought about it until now, but it must have been the sheer weight of things in his pockets that caused him to wear braces as well as a belt.

A colleague once bludgeoned him into emptying his pockets while a group of us were lunching in the office canteen of the magazine where we were working. Jock was pictorial editor. We counted 34 items. Among them, I remember, were a gadget combining pliers and screwdrivers, three magnifying glasses of different sizes and strengths, four neatly coiled lengths of string, and two compasses, one of them a metal button which, when balanced on the point of a pin or splinter of wood, indicated north. The button compass was part of Jock's escape gear should he have been shot down over Germany while flying Beaufort bombers during the Second World War. He offered no reason as to why he was still carrying it twenty-odd years later.

Stomp, stomp, stomp. . .

A large brushtail possum was marching on all fours through the living room, shoulders hunched like a bull terrier on the attack. Rummy, Jock's dog whom I called Old Untameable although he wasn't old, backed away warily; Nicky, the ginger tom, opened an eye, half closed it.

'Good evening, Nibbles. Have you come for your supper?' Jock stepped down into the living room and held out a piece of apple. The possum stood on his hind legs and, taking it gently, squatted on his hindquarters while it munched away, an eye on the other pieces of apple in Jock's hand. For the next few minutes, Jock demonstrated man's mastery over nature, moving around the living room, calling to Nibbles when he finished a piece of apple and holding another piece high above the floor so that Nibbles had to stomp across the room, stand upright, and reach for the apple rather like a dancing bear.

For Nibbles, this must have been all rather tedious. He was interested in apple, not circus tricks.

Dangling the large remaining piece of apple by the stalk at arm's length, Jock called out again. His voice had the ring of confidence of a lion tamer so convinced he has his act totally under control he has sat on his lion-tamer's chair to bask in the crowd's applause.

Nibbles looked at the apple core, licked the juice from his lips, then suddenly bounded across the room and launched himself at Jock as though he were a gum tree. The possum landed with a thump on Jock's thigh and his long claws dug in through the trousers. Jock yowled, but undeterred, Nibbles clambered upwards, his pace only marginally slowed by the yielding material.

'Off, Nibbles!' Jock roared, shedding his savoir-faire. 'Off!' But Nibbles continued to scale Jock hand over hand or rather long-clawed paw over long-clawed paw.

'Here!' Jock yelled desperately. 'Take it!' And tossed the apple core to me. I caught it by a reflex action.

Nibbles' reflexes were equally responsive. With his sights still on the apple, he launched himself from Jock's chest and bounded towards me. But I had no intention of being a possum pincushion. I darted behind a lounge chair, held out the apple for Nibbles to see clearly, then lobbed it through the open front door on to the wide verandah.

This suited Nibbles. He did a sharp left turn and rushed after it. Quickly, I shut the glass-panelled door behind him.

A brief handclap seemed appropriate. 'Performing seals next?' I asked.

'Very droll,' Jock growled, unamused. He had rolled up his trousers to inspect his leg. Apart from the pain, no lion tamer likes to get mauled: it takes the edge off the act.

There was a thump on the front door. Nibbles was squatting on his haunches peering at Jock over the edge of the timber frame along the base of the glass door. Jock had pulled out his shirt to investigate the damage the possum's claws had caused to his torso.

There was another thump on the front door. Nibbles had his shoulder to it the way I once saw John Wayne effect entry to a western saloon. 'Buzz off!' said Jock waving a hand at the door.

I felt a certain sympathy for Nibbles. He was a victim of man's contrariness and I felt I should explain this to him. I walked over to the door and addressed the possum. 'Nibbles!' I said. But he ignored me: he was staring at Jock. 'Nibbles!' I repeated to no effect, then concluded that as he was the height of my shins the message wasn't reaching him. I got down on my hands and knees to meet him eyeball to eyeball. His big dark eyes stared into mine.

'He doesn't want to play any more,' I explained through the glass, jerking my head towards Jock. 'It's a way humans have. They start the game; they finish it. Thank you for your participation.' His big ears twitched above his pretty fox-like face, his pink nose wrinkled. 'Now I suggest you go eat some gum leaves. For lettuce and apple, try again tomorrow night.'

Nibbles must have got the point. He broke eye contact, got down on all fours and walked with a rolling gait across the verandah. Then he leapt effortlessly on to the railing and swooped to a branch of the nearby jacaranda tree and could be heard making his way up one of the two giant camphor laurels that shaded the house.

'I think we need a drink,' said Jock.

'I think you need some antiseptic,' I said.

Jock grunted. 'Well, you know where everything is. I'll have a Scotch.' He lit another cigarette, then stepped down into the living room, heading for the bathroom.

'Scotch?' I said to Jean as I crossed to the cabinet on the far side of the living room.

'Not for me. I'm having a white wine.'

'Sounds fine. Would you please make that two?'

I took the bottle from the fine old cabinet, as pleasing as the other pieces of antique furniture in the large, high-ceilinged room that had such a distinctive character. It was entirely lined—ceiling and walls—with pressed-metal sheets embossed with varying flamboyant patterns. Pressed metal had been a popular material for ceilings for decades up to the 1930s but I had never before seen a room completely lined with it.

Indeed, the whole house oozed character. It had been built by theatre types early in the century when the suburb was carved out of the bush above Sydney's Middle Harbour, and sort of spread around the large central living room. Clearly, it had been built for entertaining, for fun living.

The dining area where we had been sitting had been attached to the side of the house as an afterthought. Raised a handspan above the floor of the rest of the house and with curtain track still in situ, it had been built as a stage that boasted a grand piano. World-renowned Australian opera singer Nellie Melba had sung there at weekend parties. A flat area on the hillside above us where the road now ran, had been used as a little open-air theatre with a magnificient view over the harbour.

I was fond of Jock and Jean's old house: it was my kind of house. Like Jock's pockets it was full of interesting things: a display cabinet of arrow heads made by ancient Britons, Chinese ceramics and paintings, and in his workroom an almost unbelievable collection of gadgetry, rock, mineral and gem samples, and the stark white skull, complete with a sweeping pair of horns, of a monstrous and very dead steer that he had come across on a trip out west.

Jock returned, now dismissive of his scratches and smelling

of antiseptic as well as tobacco smoke. 'Shall we move on to the verandah?' he said. He had a deliberate way of speaking, his native Scottish accent diffused by years of living in Europe and now Australia. We had lost the 'refraction-of-light-in-crystals' theme which had developed from I'm not sure what.

It was like that with Jock. The beginning of every conversation was the start of a glorious adventure into the unknown. You never knew which path you were going to take or where you'd end up.

A three-quarter moon lit the harbour, seen through the branches of two Norfolk Island pines and a giant bunya-bunya tree. On the ridge above the far shore the castellated tower of an ersatz castle—a whimsical touch of Medieval Europe set among gum trees and reeking of a colonial's homesickness years ago—stood out in isolation against a blue-black, still-starless sky. Water lapped against the rocks in the bay below us.

We sat looking at the harbour without speaking, sipping our drinks. 'Beautiful!' I finally said.

'Then you should come and live here,' said Jean. 'I don't know how you can bear the racket in town. You should rent Peterson's cottage next door.' She spoke rather imperiously: at such times her voice was very English.

'The boatshed on the waterfront?' I had seen it at a distance a number of times.

'It's not a boatshed,' said Jean emphatically. 'It was turned into a dear little cottage like ours years ago.' She was referring to a quaint house below us on the foreshore which they let. 'And it's not really Peterson's any more. People called Wilcox have just bought the property. They're an English family, not long here. I understand they'll live in the main house next door to us and rent out the cottage.'

I peered down the hillside to the left at the outline of a tiled hip roof way down by the water. 'It still looks like a boatshed.'

'A small boat can go underneath.'

'And there must be a million steps.'

7

'A hundred and fifty two to road level,' said Jock. It was the sort of thing I would expect him to know precisely.

'They're not straight up,' said Jean, reading my mind. 'They're interspersed with lengths of path.'

'And there are only 23 up to the loo,' said Jock.

'What?' I said. 'You mean it's got an outside dunny, a one-holer?'

'With a fine stained-glass window in the back wall.'

'Ahh! That's class!' I remembered he had majored in stained glass when he did his fine arts degree. 'Jock, at Rushcutters Bay I have a very fine flush loo next to the bedroom and to reach the flat I climb twelve carpeted stairs.'

'To be driven mad,' said Jean, 'by cars, buses, motor mowers and that chappie who's always welding in the yacht club workshop with his hammer going tap, tap, tap. You said so.'

She was quite right. Near-city noise was really bothering me. We hadn't discussed this, but I desperately needed a quiet place for maybe just four or five months to complete a writing project.

'Umm!' I said reflectively, and was peering down the hill-side with some interest when I remembered Elvina Bay.

Before returning to the city I had been living in an isolated spot on the Pittwater in the extreme north of the Sydney area, running a boat business in the naive belief that I would write in my spare time. Contact with the rest of the world was only by boat. This could be awkward at times—but 152 steps? No way!

Dropping an armful of blankets and pillows on the floor of the tiny bedroom at the rear of the cottage I walked through to the front and looked out over the water. Now that wasn't much bother, was it? I said to myself.

It was down hill, I muttered, and you picked the easy things first.

It had been a hectic morning; I was set to have an argument.

Are you *sure* you've made the right decision?

Sure I'm sure. At least I think I'm sure. Anyway I've signed the lease. . .Listen, it's only for six months.

I pondered on this. Six months can be an awfully long time at the bottom of a precipice, I thought glumly.

It's not a precipice; it's a slope, in parts, quite a gradual slope.

Well, you've made the decision. . .It *is* a perfect spot for writing and no one's going to rap on the wall when you practise the fiddle. That's a plus. Let's have a look at the terrace alongside the cottage. . .Very pleasant. A couple of easy chairs, a garden table and a chilled bottle of Chardonnay. . .

Okay, I might as well get on with it. Here we go. . .Two steps up, two paces along the flat. . .Jean was right. The path has been well planned; the straight flat bits provide a change of pace and enable you to get your breath. . .Four steps up, four along the flat, three steps up, three along the flat. . .

You weren't going to count, remember?

I wasn't. But I've decided I might just as well know where I am right from the start.

You said it was like the time you had surgery: you didn't want to know the details or you'd start performing your own operation in your head.

This is clearly different. . .Ah, the dunny perched on the hillside. Spot on, Jock. Twenty-three steps. I might as well have a look inside. . .*Voila*! A faithful Hygia; the Australian mechanical loo; the bushman's one luxury item! A remarkable piece of engineering. Wouldn't surprise me if it played a tune when I raise the lid. No, it doesn't, just a rattle of cogs and things. . .Umm!. . . Rattle, rattle, rattle!. . .It's percussion! Play around with the tempo a bit and it could be contemporary music. . .And the stained-glass window in the back wall! Now that *is* class in a tin shed. . .All very satisfactory. Okay, forward. . .

Thirty-three rock-carved steps later I paused for a breather in front of my new landlord's house which was level with the Muirs'. But was it really the front? I thought. The more

9

impressive facade of Don and Joyce Wilcox's house faced the harbour, but the entrance on the other side, which I saw as the back of the house, faced the road.

I looked down the hill at the cottage jutting over the cliff on the very edge of the harbour. Umm. Same situation there: I could be living back to front.

The neat cottage with its red-tiled roof was tucked between the water and the hillside. I speculated on what the building had been originally. It couldn't have been a boathouse because it was five metres above the high-tide mark. A sort of cave had been cut out of the sandstone rock underneath where a couple of dinghies or a sailing skiff could be stacked. Perhaps it had simply been built as a storage shed after which a wide verandah had been added to three sides and enclosed with windows to make it a snug weekender.

Four along the flat, two steps up. . .

Did Jock really say 152? And that's only one way. The reality is, to get all my possessions down I should double it for down then up. That's 304 steps per load. And how many trips am I likely to make to empty the car? Let's say fifteen. That's, er, 4560!

My god! Didn't you stop to think about the shopping—or garbage night? Just as well the piano's in storage.

As I climbed the path to bring down yet another carton of books I heard Jean's friendly call, 'Hi, Neighbour Fraser!'

I paused for breath on step 42 from the bottom. 'And good morning to you, Neighbour Muir.'

And that's the way it was to be for many years to come with neighbours Muir, neighbours Wilcox, neighbours Dennis, neighbours Fisher, neighbours Easton. . .

2

Gone fishin'

The position I had chosen for my desk was close to perfection: it was in the front right-hand corner of the cottage facing the lawned terrace.

Absolute perfection would have been facing the harbour, but I had reminded myself that I wasn't here on a holiday, I was here to work. Rigid discipline was to be the order of the day. There was to be no nonsense about spending valuable time 'thinking', that feeble justification of the writer for staring out of the window at passing clouds as if in expectation of the archangel Gabriel appearing with a concise story line, *and* the preparation and consumption of more liquid—in the form of cups of coffee and tea—than a camel would swallow before setting off to cross the Gobi Desert.

I had even considered putting my desk in the far corner of the living room, which was the main room in the centre of the cottage, facing a blank wall. But that would have been too much like locking myself in a monk's cell and I didn't see myself as a candidate for holy orders.

No, I would simply apply myself to putting words on paper in a professional manner, resting my eyes occasionally by glancing at the green lawn and the pleasing shape of a large coral tree at the far end of the terrace where I had already decided to build a barbecue.

Should I feel tempted to look to my left to critically assess the three boats moored in the bay or find myself looking along the wooded shoreline that ran off at a right-angle to the north speculating on what lay around the corner of the distant point I could always draw the curtains.

So I applied myself to my work to the accompaniment of lapping water, bird calls, the rustle of leaves and occasionally the thin, distant sound of a lone car.

By mid-morning I felt that I could take a break with an easy conscience. I brewed coffee in the kitchen, which was on the other side of the cottage, and took a couple of turns along by the front windows like Nelson on his poop deck, admiring the three-sided view while I stretched my legs. Sydney can be sublime in early winter with cloudless skies and a warm gentle sun that silvers the harbour.

I propped my arms on a window sill and looked down at the jetty which extended from the cave-like area under the cottage. Some months previously, missing the water after selling the boat business, I had bought a 3.6-metre sailing boat which I transported on a trailer. It would be quite a simple matter, I thought, to build a light slipway alongside the jetty which would enable me draw my little boat under the house leaving it partly rigged ready for sailing.

As I looked down, several sizable bream swam from under the jetty and began nibbling at the oysters on the rocks right below me. I gulped. It was almost too good to be true. I remembered my fishing rod was lying on top of several cartons of books in the living room. I went to the refrigerator, carved a couple of slivers off a piece of meat, grabbed the fishing rod and hurried through the kitchen door and down the steps to the jetty.

The fish had swum off by the time I got there and I guessed they had gone to deeper water. I walked to the end of the jetty and cast. Not half an hour, but half a minute later I had a strike.

A beautiful silver bream!

I'm made! I thought joyfully. Immediate visions of an idyllic existence, living, not on the smell of an oily rag that had all too often been my lot as a writer, but on fresh fish—fried, grilled, baked, steamed—preceded by entrees of superb oysters that were growing by the thousands on the rocks around me, and mussels clinging to the jetty piles.

I took my catch upstairs, put it in the refrigerator and returned to my desk, glowing. I had only to buy the potatoes.

At the end of the most successful working day I had enjoyed in months I rewarded myself by pouring a glass of beer and wandering down to the jetty where I sat with my legs swinging above the water. Sipping my beer, I let my eyes wander over the hillsides rising from the rocky foreshore, admiring the exotically twisting limbs of the pink-trunked angophoras, close relatives of nearby eucalypts, the clumps of native pines and she-oaks, and the scattering of houses half-hidden among the trees.

The cottage was nestled in a bay fed by a freshwater creek that tumbled through a pocket of subtropical rainforest to my right at the head of the bay. A giant fig tree and several species of palm tree lined the creek bank.

I already knew that the bay had a nice touch of history. Years before, hulks used for storing the colony's blasting powder had been moored here in this remote corner of the harbour. Even now, it was still out of the mainstream although, off-peak, the city was only twenty minutes away by car. One of the boats moored in the bay was the tender used by the sailing club whose clubhouse was several hundred metres away on the northern side of the creek.

The cottage to my left was another converted boatshed which was built right out over the water on sandstone foundations. Lorna Dennis was coming down the long flight of wooden stairs that had been built to get past the vertical rock face that formed a natural wall at the back of her garden. She appeared to be loaded like a prospector's mule and for good measure had a little girl attached to each hand. She detached a hand and waved.

'Hi, Neighbour Dennis!' I called.

Lorna's husband, Ross, was a long-distance truck driver. Only hardy souls would brave the bearing and raising of children on a block of land that would be considered ideal territory by a chamois goat. The hillside steepened even more as it progressed south-west along the shoreline. Where there were particularly steep pinches, spiral staircases had been installed for access to the cottages down by the water.

The far side of the harbour was a kilometre or so away at the nearest point. The area to the left was quite heavily built on, although it had been kept well treed, with some fine houses rising up the slope to the horizon now reddened by the lowering sun. The remaining area to the right beyond the headland was still virgin bush. My map showed me long arms of water and bays waiting to be explored. It was all wonderfully peaceful.

I was examining clusters of mussels on the piles with a view to whipping up a delicious Italian recipe I have for mussel soup when a large leatherjacket swam sluggishly from under the jetty and dawdled around beneath my feet.

Tomorrow night's dinner!

It wasn't so much a matter of casting, as dangling the baited hook in front of the fish.

Now leatherjackets, which look rather like a flatfish such as a flounder or sole that has suddenly, to its surprise, found itself swimming vertically, can be tricky to catch. They have very small mouths and so are attracted to delicate portions of bait. Apart from which they are finnicky.

Time and again the leatherjacket approached the bait with seeming interest, gave it a nudge with its fluted snout—and floated away.

Leatherjacket was off the menu.

The next day, the same fish, I assumed, was still there under the jetty, its little snout going ga-bloop, ga-bloop like a goldfish in a tank.

I bought some very small hooks.

But day followed day with the leatherjacket blowing bubbles, ga-blooping and merely sniffing at tempting morsels of prawn and a range of enticing fish bait. I felt I was being challenged: my hunting instincts were by now well and truly aroused.

I bought a fish spear.

Jock and Jean Muir were my first dinner guests. Both commented that the several varieties of fish arranged attractively on a platter in the centre of the table looked delicious and Jock, a keen fisherman, began questioning me about just where I had cast, the bait I had used, the tides, and such piscatorial matters.

I replied, as I served and placed their plates before them, 'I caught the bream and the flathead from the end of the jetty, the bream quite well out, and the flathead closer in, in shallower water toward your place. The leatherjacket, I must confess, I speared in a most unsportsmanlike way.'

'Speared?' said Jock, looking down at the leatherjacket pan-fried golden brown before him.

'Yes.' I nodded toward the harbour. 'A tricky angle shot under the jetty.'

Jock had picked up his knife and fork. 'Under the jetty?'

'Yes. Took me several days, but I got him.'

Jock put down his knife and fork. 'Lennie,' he said, '*lived* under the jetty.'

Oh no! I thought. Like Nibbles the possum in the ceiling!

Jock passed me his plate. 'Would you mind if I had the bream?' And added as we made the exchange, 'It might be better if we didn't tell the children.'

So I ate Lennie. I felt like a cannibal.

'Now do be careful,' said my landlord, whom I had dubbed the Squire, from the other side of the drawn curtains as he climbed over the terrace fence to the scaffolding he had erected across the front of the cottage. Don Wilcox was a meticulous man, with a nice, quirky sense of humour.

'I'm always careful,' said Walter, seen through a chink, heaving his stocky bulk after him.

'You're not, you know.'

'Oh yes, I am. I was painting on scaffolding before you were born.'

'I expect you were; you're my father.'

'Then just remember it,' said Walter.

'Well *you* remember that you're five metres up,' said Squire Wilcox.

'Might as well be a hundred. Anyway, we're over water.'

'Watch it, Dad! You nearly slipped!'

'I never slip.'

'You forget your age, that's your trouble.'

'Haven't forgot a birthday yet, and I've had 78 of them.'

'Be careful stirring that paint. I wish you'd wear a safety rope.'

'A *safety* rope? I can swim.'

'But what if you have a heart attack?'

'I never have heart attacks.'

3

Give a dog a bad name. . .

'You have only to say no and we'll try to make other arrangements,' said Jock.

'Not at all,' I said. 'Not at all.'

'The problem is when we go bush that if anyone recognises. . .'

'Jock, I really would like to look after him. He'll be no trouble, I assure you.'

'Well, you have only to say. . .'

'Jock!'

So when the time came for the Muirs to leave on another of their gem-fossicking expeditions, just before departure Jock came down to the cottage, big boots clomping, big bush hat on his head, carrying his dog's personal effects. Rummy trotted at his heels. Jock had brought Rummy's food bowl, an ample supply of provisions, his sleeping rug, chain and muzzle.

If I had thought about it at all, I had visualised the dog sleeping by the door, but Jock spread the rug beside my desk as though it were the preordained place for him to be and put his effects neatly beside the rug.

Rummy watched this with interest. He was a handsome dog, similar to and almost the size of an Alsation but a little lighter in build. His head was well set, his ears were pricked, his eyes bright, intelligent. 'Sit, Rummy,' said Jock, jabbing a forefinger at the rug, and Rummy sat looking up at Jock who, dressed for the bush, was bulging even more than usual; that is, the pockets of his baggy shorts and safari jacket were bulging even more than usual; packed with indispensible things. 'Now you are staying with Bryce.' Pointing at me. 'I wish I could take you with me, but you know I can't. You *stay* here. *Stay!* And be a good dog.'

Rummy remained sitting while Jock made his farewells with me, then with a final 'Stay!' went out through the door and closed it behind him. Rummy sat with head cocked to one side, pricked ears listening to Jock's boots clomping up the stone steps. Then suddenly he moved swiftly and silently and stood with his nose to the crack in the door. He whimpered and looked up at the Yale lock set high in the door, then stood on his hind legs and tried to reach the doorknob with his forepaws.

'You won't make it, Rummy,' I said. 'It's too high and anyway the knob's too small.' He'd already found this out and his forepaws slid down the door until he stood on all four legs. The scratch marks from his claws were quite marginal, but the attempt didn't bode well.

'Listen, Old Untameable,' I said. 'I think we had better have an understanding. I'm only the tenant here and I don't think Squire Wilcox will appreciate having his front door shredded. When you're in, you're in, okay?'

But I knew this wasn't Rummy's philosophy as witnessed by the scratch marks gouged in the door of Jock's workroom at the rear of the Muirs' house where Rummy was sometimes locked in. The door was bolted from the inside room. The key for the worn old lock, which coincidentally was set in the door only a little above Rummy's nose height, had long since been lost and Rummy could open the unbolted door by giving the large brass knob an eighth turn with both forepaws and pushing.

This tactility was typical of the breed. To watch Rummy eating a bone held upright between his paws you would think he was manipulating chopsticks.

Judging that the sound of Jock's footsteps must by now be

beyond the range of the dog's hearing I decided that it was time to establish discipline. I glanced apprehensively at the muzzle among Rummy's effects then called in a strict-but-fair voice, 'Rummy!' He turned his head. 'Stay, Rummy!' I jabbed my forefinger at the rug. 'Sit.'

I thought I detected an 'and-just-who-do-you-think-you're-talking-to' glint in his eye as he thought about this for a long moment, but after a final glance at the crack of light coming through the edge of the door he walked back to his rug and lay down, his long snout on his forepaws, eyes still on the door.

So far so good. I considered moving rug, dog and effects to the spot I had had in mind, then rationalised that if this was the spot where Rummy had been told to stay, best he stayed. I had no wish to rock the boat.

I sat down again at my desk looking at the animal I was nominally in charge of for the next few weeks. I say nominally because there was the off-chance that Rummy could be in charge of me.

Up until now, I had had what might be termed a nodding acquaintance with Rummy. Invariably, I had seen him in company with a member of his family and our relationship had been cordial. While I patted his head I had remained a little wary.

Looking at him, I thought, Umm, there's no mistaking him: no wonder Jock doesn't care to take him bush. He stands out like a sore thumb—reddish-yellow coat, white paws, white tail tip. The classic features. Although they're not all that colour. I've seen them sort of black and I believe there are some piebald and yellow-white. His mother, of course, was pure white and beautiful.

When asked what breed Rummy was Jock would say gravely, 'He's a rum one. A Tibetan wolfhound. They're rather rare here.' When pushed into a corner by the more knowing he would concede, 'He's probably a kelpie cross.' Then with his back on the ropes would protest defensively, 'They're only a dog; they're classified *Canis familiaris.*'

But he dropped a word. Rummy was *Canis familiaris dingo,*

an Australian native dog. As such, his reputation was that he was untameable, a cunning, ruthless killer of sheep and calves. He was regarded by governments as vermin, and he was the target of bounty hunters. Even here in suburbia he had a price on his scalp.

I worked away for an hour or so then became aware of Rummy standing at the door. The quietness with which dingoes move can be a little unnerving. It's very much a matter of, Ah, there you are; Oh, there you're not. This is the more remarkable because their claws are not retractable.

'Do you want to go outside?' I said, whereupon he glanced at me then looked up at the doorknob expectantly. This wasn't quite to plan. 'When he wants to go outside he'll bring you his muzzle,' Jock had said, and had convinced me over the previous week that Rummy would, in fact, pick up his muzzle and take it to the nearest person to have it fitted so that he could go for a stroll.

'Haven't you forgotten something?' I said, pointing to his personal effects beside my desk. 'How about your muzzle?'

He continued to look up at the doorknob. 'So!' I said. 'Is this a try on? Are you testing me?' And I picked up the muzzle and swung it casually for him to see. He displayed no interest.

Why the muzzle? Well, most houses throughout the suburb were unfenced and when Rummy went outside he had the run of the district. I had mentioned to Jock that the sight of a large muzzled dog on the loose could be off-putting to many people and he had been quite offended. 'Rummy wouldn't bite anyone,' he said. And in fact, in the wild there have been few unprovoked attacks by dingoes on human beings.

But the truth is, Rummy wasn't exactly squeaky clean. He was top dog of the district and naturally you don't get to wear the champ's belt without ripping an ear or two. Then there was the chicken stealing and the humiliation of being chained up in the garden with a dead chicken tied around your neck. (What Rummy actually learned from this was that a smart dog doesn't bring home the chickens he catches.) And there was the four-legged lawnmower bought by the Muirs' neighbour on the other side. Bruce Pearce tied the sheep to a stake which he moved around the hillside so that the grass was evenly cropped. To Rummy and Bruce's labrador, Blackie, who was Rummy's mate, this was manna from dingo heaven. . .

Jock reasoned that the muzzle was a means of ensuring Rummy's survival in suburbia. If he couldn't grab a dog's ear or a chicken's wing or a sheep's hind leg he couldn't be accused of misdeeds.

So Jock had given me a course of instruction on putting the muzzle on Rummy, saying, 'He really doesn't mind it as it means he can go for a walk.'

But I had gained the distinct impression that while Rummy accepted the muzzle as a matter of necessity when put on by a member of his family, he wasn't at all keen on the device, particularly when it was fitted by a mere acquaintance. It was rather like putting a bridle on a spirited, strange horse you've just been given to ride. In the fitting, I had the opportunity of seeing Rummy's fine set of teeth at close quarters.

It was apparent that I had to adopt a firm stand from scratch. 'No muzzle,' I said, 'no walk.' And sat down again at my desk and began typing.

Soon I felt my knee being nudged. Rummy was standing patiently beside me, his muzzle between his jaws. I put it on him without difficulty, attached the muzzle strap to a safety clip on his collar and opened the door for him.

He returned some time later laughing happily the way dogs do as he came inside. He was no longer wearing his muzzle: it hung from the collar clip, dangling between his forelegs like a Scotsman's sporran. How had he got it off? How many Pekingese and Australian terrier corpses were strewn around the streets? Momentarily, I felt a sense of failure as a dingo minder. Here I was on Day One and the ground rules had already been blown apart. Eyeing Rummy from a respectful distance I could see no splashes of blood, i.e., Pekingese and terrier blood.

In fact, he looked rather ridiculous standing there with his

sporran. He must have felt so too because he walked up to me, raised a white paw and tapped my leg. I took this as a request and unclipped the muzzle. He then settled contentedly on his rug beside my desk.

Normally, I avoid doing business in pubs, but by coincidence a scientist engaged on a research program on crocodiles in the Northern Territory lived a suburb or two away and I had arranged to interview him for an hour late that afternoon in a local hostelry. I had forgotten I would be acting as deputy master to a dingo.

When it was time for me to go, Rummy appeared to be sound asleep on his rug so I decided to run the risk of having the door shredded and leave him inside. However, he raised his head when he heard the latch click. 'Stay!' I said, raising a finger the way Jock did. 'I'll be back soon.' He seemed to nod approval.

The interview went extremely well and the planned one hour slipped away as the scientist talked on about Australia's man-eating crocodiles with which he seemed to have an improbable love affair. It was pitch dark and I was without a torch as I threaded my way down the hill. My head was still full of stories of the guile of crocodiles, of how a croc will patiently watch someone draw a bucket of water from a river at roughly the same time day after day, then suddenly—*wham!*—it will leap from beneath the river bank with startling speed and grab its victim in its great jaws.

I opened the door and was fumbling for the light switch when suddenly my left wrist was clamped in a vice-like grip.

My head screamed, '*Crocodiles!*' and I tried to tear my arm away as my other hand found the switch.

But my arm wasn't going anywhere. Rummy was standing just inside the door, my wrist in his mouth. Blinking in the light, I stood very still as my head scrambled between panic and relief, pointlessly endeavouring to evaluate the relative menace of crocodiles and dingoes.

There was no sound or sensation of crunching bone. Indeed, the grip of his jaws was merely firm. His eyes seemed friendly.

'It's all right, Rummy,' I said, my voice a marginally higher pitch than usual. 'It's me, your deputy master.'

His tail wagged: he knew this.

'Okay, then. You can let go now. I'm not a burglar.'

He wagged his tail again.

Then I remembered. 'Rummy's easygoing about most things,' Jock had said. 'But he insists on having his dinner at sundown.'

'So you want your dinner, Old Untameable,' I said jovially. At least I hoped I sounded jovial, and as his jaws were already occupied thought it safe to pat him tentatively on the top of his head. 'Okay, just let me go and I'll get it for you.'

But it seemed that Rummy had heard that sort of promise before. His jaws remained clamped around my wrist; the grip wasn't painful, just firm, very firm.

'All right,' I said, 'let's go into the kitchen, shall we? Let's get your dinner.' And I walked, dingo attached, towards the kitchen. His dinner, which Jean cooked in the belief that this would develop a more sophisticated palate for food other than wild game, was in the refrigerator.

I opened the refrigerator door with my free hand and held out the dish of stewed scrag-end of mutton for him to inspect, much like a waiter proferring a fine vintage for a diner's approval. His eyes said, 'Great! A good year. Let's have a taste.' He remained attached.

I put the bowl on the floor and only then did he relax his grip. He wagged his tail and sat down in front of it, licking his lips. I wondered if he was waiting for me to say grace. Then I remembered Jock's formal discipline. Rummy was not permitted to start eating until Jock gave the word. 'Okay, Rummy,' I said. 'Dinner!' And he moved forward quickly toward the bowl. But then he ate quite slowly and deliberately: he was not a greedy dog.

The scene in the cottage that night was one of near domestic bliss. I sat in a comfortable chair reading, dog at my feet, dreaming, as indicated by twitching nose and rapid little running movements of all four feet. All that was needed to complete the cliché, I thought, were carpet slippers, a pipe and a good woman with knitting needles clicking in another corner of the room.

Foolishly, I let the cliché take over. Not that I could recall Mandy ever knitting a sweater. Now that sounds unfair. It's just that it started me thinking again. Thinking's bad. Once a marriage is over there's no point in thinking. No children to compound the agony. Decisions made. Action taken. End of story. Cut.

Well, that's the theory.

Then I got it into my head that the boats had become my children; *mine*, not ours. And a demanding bunch of 'kids' they were. But I jumped on that notion with both feet, turned a page and got on with my reading.

At the end of a chapter I put down my book and spent a minute or two inspecting Rummy. He certainly was a handsome dog, bigger and fitter than the dingoes I'd encountered in the bush. But then, he was the second generation to be raised in the relative comfort of a private zoo with a roof over

Give a dog a bad name. . .

his head and a square meal every day. He didn't know what it was to have to trot mile after mile in the hope of catching a kangaroo, a rabbit or a lizard.

In the dreaming, Rummy's mouth twitched giving glimpses of his fine set of teeth. But he actually had been quite gentle, I mused. Had he harboured malice for being served dinner later than usual he could have crunched my wrist with relative ease. I winced at the thought and made a mental note not to walk around with my arms dangling at sunset. It might even be best if I adopted the habit of folding them in the late afternoon.

After all, I continued to muse, he's only a dog. He was the Aborigines' dog before the tribes were shattered by European settlement. What a pity he can't be recognised as such, Australia's very own breed, which would spare Jock the nonsense of having to swear to everyone that he's a genuine Tibetan wolfhound to save his scalp. But the breed does have a rather nasty reputation. My curiosity aroused, I got up and took volume 2 of *The Australian Encyclopaedia* from the bookshelf.

Between the 'Dimboola' and 'Dinosaurs' entries I read, 'DINGO or Warrigal, a feral species of the genus *Canis*, widely distributed over the Australian continent but not in Tasmania. It is generally believed to have evolved from a domesticated version of the Asiatic wolf, or the Indian wild dog (*dhole*) which accompanied the. . .Aborigines. . .[to]. . .Australia. . .'

So, Rummy, you're not a true-blue Aussie, but an Asian migrant—accepting a settling-in period of a few thousand years.

'. . .The dingo's strong carnassial teeth (rear premolars) and habit of silent hunting are wolf-like characteristics, while the inability to bark—it utters a drawn-out howl—indicates the primitive origin. . .'

I could vouch for the strong carnassial teeth.

'. . .Dingoes usually hunt alone or in pairs, showing great cunning in following drovers for weeks in order to pick up any straggling stock; in rounding up sheep for a mass killing; in accustoming a cow to their presence and then seizing her calf; in trailing wallabies to trap a young one or a weakling; or in attacking large kangaroos, one seizing the tail, and the other the throat. . .'

In other words, Rummy, you're a survivor.

It got nastier, detailing the incredible numbers of livestock alleged to have been killed by dingoes, and the measures taken to control them. '. . .To contain dingoes, barrier fences have been erected over vast areas, and trapping, shooting and poisoning are employed. . .'

Best you stay put in suburbia, Old Untameable. And take my tip, don't get too tetchy come sundown. It's a tough world out there.

'Rummy! This is for your own good. . .*Rummy!* Keep still or I'll poke your eye out. . .*R-u-m-m-y!*' Kneeling on the floor I had him in a headlock. It was like wrestling a furry eel. There was a knock on the door. '*Come in!*' I roared in the same voice.

The door opened a little and a friend's neatly bearded face appeared in the gap. 'What's going on?'

'No time to explain. I'm in the middle of round three with Rummy.'

Robert stepped inside, his blue eyes considering me quizzically. 'I think he's winning.'

'No way,' I said. 'So far I've come out on top every time.'

Just then Rummy stopped wriggling to look up at Robert and I squeezed the tube, squirting the ointment right into his eye. 'Got him! Round three to the man in the blue trunks!' I let Rummy go and he stood there rubbing his eye with a paw. 'Good boy. Spread the ointment around. Remember, same time same place tomorrow.' And by way of explanation to Robert, 'An old wound from a scrap he once had with a possum. It flared up, so I took him to the vet who prescribed this performance daily. I need one of those weapons of yours to bail him up in a corner.'

Robert laid his fencing foils on the table; it seemed he had been spending the early part of the evening dancing around on his nimble feet endeavouring to skewer someone in a vital part. He bent over to ruffle Rummy's ears. 'But why aren't you applying Pavlov's theory?' he said.

'What's bell ringing got to do with it?' I said, wiping a misdirected squirt of ointment from a shirt cuff.

'I wouldn't put it like that,' Robert said icily. 'I'm sorry, but you're simply going about it the wrong way.'

'I won't argue with you.' Robert is very good at this sort of thing. He's a lecturer in communication and various other subjects and has a way with furred and feathered creatures as well as the human species when he's not trying to skewer them. 'The question is, what's the right way?'

'As I said, the Pavlov theory. Has he had his dinner?'

'Yep, a few minutes ago. No bothers there—provided I'm right on the knocker.'

'Then you're too late. You're doing things back to front. As you no doubt recall, the theory is based on pairing an uncon-ditioned natural stimulus with a conditioned or learned stimulus.'

'Huh?' I said.

'Terrible language,' said Robert, 'but that's the way they put it. You pair a familiar behaviour pattern, such as being excited by food, with an unfamiliar one, such as open your eye so I can squirt in some ointment.' Robert's an articulate fellow, which I guess is one of the reasons he's a lecturer.

'How about the bell ringing?'

'That comes later. What is fascinating about Ivan Petrovich Pavlov's theory is not simply that a dog is persuaded to accept something for the reward—you can get almost anyone to do almost anything if the reward is great enough—but that instinctive behaviour is blended with unnatural behaviour. You know, Pavlov's work early this century paved the way for the modern psychology of behaviourism.' Robert paused and stroked his pointed beard. Perhaps he saw my eyes glazing over. 'Normally I charge a fat fee to lecture on this sort of thing. Would you like me to come by tomorrow night? I'll demonstrate it to you for a steak.'

'You mean you're volunteering to play shrink?'

'If you'd like me to.'

'It's a deal. A steak and three veg—and I'll throw in a glass of red.'

'Done. But don't feed him before I arrive. His dinner is *his* reward.'

My friend returned late the following afternoon just as Rummy was giving clear hints that something was expected of me in the kitchen. It was dangerously close to nightfall. 'Hello, boy,' said Robert, ruffling Rummy's ears to reinforce their friendly relationship. I thought he was taking a risk at this late hour but I hadn't told him of Rummy's penchant for clamping his jaws on the hand that fed him.

I had everything ready on the kitchen bench. 'The finest scrag-end of mutton,' I said, indicating Rummy's bowl, 'prepared with infinite care and served with scads of gravy. He's very fond of gravy; doubtless it will help win your way to his heart. And here's the tube of ointment. Now I want a clean fight. No kicking, gouging or biting—that particularly applies to you, Rummy—and with luck, Robert, he won't be able to break out of the clinches. I'll act as second for both of you. This'll put Ivan Petrovich Pavlov to the test. Here we go— Round one.' And I belted a saucepan lid with a spoon like a gong.

Robert had tended to ignore all this. He picked up the food bowl and the tube of ointment, it seemed to me, oozing self-confidence. I had only the vaguest idea what his job of lecturing in communication involved but it was clear that he was intent on getting through to the dingo. 'Time for dinner, boy,' he said, holding up the bowl.

Rummy stood expectantly in front of him, staring up at the bowl and licking his lips. In his book, it was way past time for dinner. Robert then put the bowl behind his back out of sight and held up the tube of ointment. 'But first the ointment in your eye. Ointment, then dinner.' Showing him the tube, then the bowl. 'Understand? Ointment *then* dinner.'

Rummy gave a whimper of expectation: clearly, he understood the dinner bit. Addressing me, Robert said, 'It probably will be just as tough tonight, but tomorrow will be different.' He knelt down on the floor holding the tube of ointment in his right hand and put his left arm around Rummy's neck. Robert was fast, but not fast enough with the headlock. With a squirm, a head shake and full thrust with his hind legs, Rummy was free.

'First point to the dingo,' I said.

Robert let this pass. 'I'll take it slowly,' he said. He picked a piece of meat from the bowl, held it up for Rummy to see, then put it back in the bowl. It occurred to me that had Rummy decided to lunge, Robert could have lost his forearm.

Robert now put his arm loosely around Rummy's neck in a friendly way and held the tube of ointment close to the dingo's eye so that he could see it very clearly. Rummy immediately backed off. Robert picked out another small piece of meat but this time he gave it to Rummy. It disappeared in a gulp.

'This is establishing the pattern,' said Robert. 'The trick is to stimulate hunger, not satisfy it.' And he repeated the sequence several times, giving Rummy a small piece of meat on each occasion. Rummy appeared puzzled by this piecemeal approach to eating even though he was not like most dogs who tend to suck up their food like an industrial vacuum cleaner.

Then Robert rumpled Rummy's ears, smartly slammed on a headlock, and to his credit, for someone who would weigh in as a lightweight, gave quite a commendable performance of dingo wrestling, cutting perhaps twelve seconds off my best time. He was wearing as much ointment as Rummy, but a squirt had hit the target.

After only a couple of pats at his eye with his paw, Rummy was looking expectantly at his food bowl and Robert.

'Good dog,' said Robert, and he went through the presentation sequence to reinforce it before putting the food bowl on the floor.

The next night Robert repeated the tube-then-bowl performance and surprisingly the tussle was minimal. 'It is tempting,' he said, watching Rummy eating his dinner with even more appreciation than usual, 'to follow through with the Pavlovian experiment.'

'That's the bell-ringing bit?'

'Yes. With the dog salivating in anticipation of food Pavlov rang a bell just before presenting it with dinner. His theory rested on the notion that the new stimulus, in the form of the bell, must be produced just before the response, which was the presentation of food. In time, the dog salivated on the ringing of the bell without being rewarded.'

'You're a braver man than me if you try that with Rummy. When he's ready for dinner he *gets* his dinner.'

'Just a thought.'

The third night was almost a pushover. Rummy gave no more than a few wriggles as Robert squirted the ointment into his eye.

On the fourth night, Robert picked up the tube, showed it to Rummy and stood waiting. The dingo made his pre-dinner whimpering noises, then trotted up, tilted back his head and stood quietly while Robert applied the ointment.

After that Rummy tucked into his dinner.

Old Untameable!

I knew at the time it was wrong: I never should have counted the steps. But it was too late now. I had made the appalling discovery that the head—my head, anyway—is locked into leg movements and clicks over like a talking odometer. Left leg up, left leg forward, 'One' says my head; right leg up, right leg forward, 'two' says my head; and so on, and so on.

Whenever I was leaving the cottage I made it a point to read the last few paragraphs I had written and concentrate purposefully on what might possibly be coming next. This was intended to jam the talking odometer as effectively as a counter-espionage radio signal. Sometimes it worked, but invariably the mind slipped off the subject and there was my head saying 'One, two, three, four. . .' and doing subtraction sums, taking the figure at the time I paused to admire the view from the total of 152. The concern was not the number of steps I had already climbed, but the number that still lay ahead. On bad days I might have been climbing Everest.

So here I was in the early morning on a simple mission to purchase a loaf of bread, a handful of Brussel sprouts, a jar of mustard pickles, a roll of sticky tape, a brace of lamb chops for myself and a kilo of neck of beef for the dingo, a diverse shopping list, but one that could be fulfilled in the compact local shopping centre within half an hour. That was the time I had allowed myself to get back to my desk and on with the job.

Reaching the roadway, taking deep, deliberate breaths which I had found effective in suppressing a physical condition that could be misinterpreted as panting, I slipped my right hand into the side pocket of my trousers for the car keys. My fingers encountered a modest amount of small change and a digestive tablet. In turn, my hands explored the left pocket of my trousers, the fob pocket and the two inaptly named hip pockets—which actually are to port and starboard over the backside—fruitlessly.

With a commendable show of patience I turned and walked back down the steps.

Keys in hand, and with my mind locked into the intricacies of the story I was working on, I again made my way to the car. Halfway to the shopping centre it seeped through my head that my exploring fingers had not encountered my wallet in my misnamed right hip pocket.

'That's nothing,' the butcher said cheerily some time later. 'The record I've heard is four trips up and down and up before a Ratty got up here to post a letter. If I was living down there I'd go through a check list like a Boeing pilot before I took off.'

'Ratty?' I queried.

'Yep. Ratty—that's what we call you waterfronters. Haven't you read *Wind in the Willows*?'

'Water rats,' said a distinguished looking elderly man standing next to me in a tone that implied suspicion of madness. 'That's what I've heard them called. I thought it was because they lived down there with the water rats. Place is alive with them, they tell me.'

Now I had seen a couple of large rat-like creatures scampering over the rocks on the foreshore and had wondered just what they were. So I asked the distinguished looking man whether they were native marsupial rats or the descendants of the common European rats that had made their way ashore down ships' mooring lines.

'God knows,' he said. 'They're all rats to me. Mind you, I've never seen them. Where are you living?'

'You're pretty well neighbours, Roy,' the butcher volunteered. 'He's next to the Muirs.'

'You know the Muirs?' I asked.

'Yes, I do,' he replied thoughtfully. 'But not very well. They're on the other side of the road, you see.'

And he explained that he lived opposite, on the high side of the road near the crown of the ridge that ran above the harbour. Then his eyes twinkled and he added, 'I burrow around in my garden, so I suppose that makes me Mole.'

The implication was not that Jock and Jean Muir were 'on the wrong side of the tracks', but that they were of an entirely different world. The Muirs were not only on the other side of the road—they were down the hill. Those on the high side of the road drove their cars to the front door and stepped inside. Those over the road and down the hill parked their cars by the side of the road or off the road on flattened bits of hillside, picked up their parcels and briefcases, perhaps slung haversacks on their backs, then disappeared from sight.

Ratties? We might have been lemmings leaping over a hundred-metre-high cliff.

I know myself sufficiently well to be aware of certain characteristics, even frailties. I know that some people see me as a detailed planner, finetuning to the point of exasperation; others, see me charging at life with reckless abandon. It even confuses me: I know I work both ways and I'm never sure just how I'm going to react when.

My agreement to be minder to a dingo falls into the second category. 'No worries, Jock,' I said, falling for the phrase that most commonly trips off Australian lips, and is the first thing to be learned by our migrants after they have mastered 'Yes'. . . 'No'. . .and 'Where is it?' I have heard 'No worries, mate' spoken in every conceivable accent and with such confidence that it comes as a shock to learn that this is almost the sole contribution that the Greek, Korean, Vietnamese or Turkish newcomer you are talking to can make to the conversation in English.

To this point, in agreeing to care for Rummy I had given no thought to what 'care' entailed. I could sit at my desk for days tapping at the typewriter oblivious to the outside world; at other times, I would be darting hither and yon gathering material and doing heaven knows what. I suppose I thought of Rummy just doing what he did normally, trotting around the district doing his rounds but spending the greater part of his time lying around at home. My role would be that of companion-cook, wroughting magic with his neck of beef and scrag-end of mutton.

The thing is, that with his family of four the chances were that there was someone at home for much of the time. But I lived alone; when I was out that was it. And as luck would have it, at this time I was darting around in an 'out' phase.

The muzzling compounded the problem. I couldn't go off for the day leaving Rummy to roam around muzzled. He found it difficult to drink and even if I left out his evening meal he wouldn't be able to eat it. I didn't like my chances of finding a volunteer among the neighbours to muzzle and unmuzzle him.

I considered the following alternatives: if I reneged on my undertaking to Jock not to let him out unmuzzled and his dinner wasn't forthcoming on the dot at dusk, I saw myself being responsible for the demise of an untold number of local livestock; if I left him locked in the house all day I could return to find it in tatters; and if I chained him up outside on the terrace I was sure he would protest in no uncertain terms.

The dingo howl is unmistakable. It is long, drawn-out, to the city dweller, eerie, chilling. As the dingo can't bark continuously like other canines, the howl is its means of communicating. I've camped in remote valleys in central Australia where the night has been filled with drawn-out howls building one upon the other like some unearthly choir as dingo has answered the call of dingo from the rocky escarpment high above me. And I've camped by a billabong in the Northern Territory where a pack of dingoes has formed a semicircle a couple of hundred metres back from the fire and howled at each other hour after hour.

I felt that to chain Rummy up for the day would not be in his interests or that of the community. So I decided the only thing was to take him with me. Rummy was, after all, *Canis familiaris*, and like all dogs he loved riding in cars. I spread his rug on the back seat, put in his chain, bowl, a bottle of water and his evening meal and headed off.

I had expected my first meeting to last half an hour; it took nearly half a day. Time ticked by. I couldn't just walk out saying, 'Sorry, I've got to go see about a dingo.' Considering the needs of nature, I had alternate images of the dog sitting cross-legged on the back seat and of shredded upholstery with the floor awash.

As I approached the car near to lunchtime I could see no sign of frenzied activity in the mobile kennel; in fact, no sign of Rummy at all. Had he shot straight through a window?

I peered inside. He was stretched full length across the car, dozing on the floor. And this set the pattern for the next few weeks. He came with me everywhere, often from early morning until late at night. He waited patiently in the car which I took care to park in shade with the windows partly wound down, would go for a run when I let him out and return immediately to my whistle, dined à la sidewalk every evening at dusk and had frequent treats of ice-cream and dog biscuits. I think he came to see himself as a dog about town.

His manners were impeccable. It wasn't just that he was obedient; he seemed to know instinctively what was expected of him.

Rummy was on his rug beside my desk when he heard, long before me, the sound of Jock Muir's big bush boots clumping down the steps. Immediately, he was at the door, nose to the crack.

'How did it go?' Jock asked anxiously before he put down the sack of rock samples he had brought to show me.

I lifted my shoulders in a shrug. 'No worries,' I said.

4

An extraordinarily large seagull

I first saw her when I glanced out of the front window one morning; she was swimming with a flock of seagulls. That's an extraordinarily large seagull, I thought, and stopped typing in mid-sentence, which wasn't difficult: the sentence wasn't getting far anyway. I propped up my chin with a fist in order to enjoy a few minutes' distraction more comfortably and watched her swimming around near the end of the jetty. Well, hardly swimming. Rather, she was just floating about; the human equivalent probably would be treading water.

No, I thought, you're definitely not a seagull. You're more like an albatross. But you're pure white. Are albatrosses (is that the plural?) pure white? I think they're well splattered with grey. You look. . .you look more like a Muscovy duck. Odd! How does a Muscovy duck come to be cruising around Sydney Harbour.

To settle the question I called to her through the window, 'Hey! You out there! You, swimming with the seagulls! Are you a duck?'

The seagulls squawked, but she didn't answer. She merely cocked her head to one side and fixed me with one little eye. But I had no intention of being trapped into a game of I-can-outstare-you, at least not by a duck. Instead, I looked her over deliberately from stem to stern, which is to say, from beak to tail tip, and pondered: Muscovy ducks, are they a wild or domestic breed? Where did this one come from—if it is a Muscovy duck? Has it migrated from the Antarctic? No, that can't be right. It's spring now, and with summer coming, if it were migrating in any direction, it would be back to the Antarctic. Perhaps it's on its way there. Or is it simply an escapee from a Sunday dinner table?

The unfinished sentence on the sheet of paper which curled out of my old typewriter nudged the corner of my eye offensively, so I twisted the roller backward smartly and the unfinished sentence, blackened with xxxxx's as though it had just passed through the hands of a particularly stringent censor, disappeared. I hate rush jobs, and mentally I gave myself another kick for accepting this one. I had completed the big project that had drawn me to the tranquillity of the bay some months back and was now writing magazine stories on assignment. Defiantly, I continued to speculate on the identity of the giant among the seagulls. She just sat there on the water, and it occurred to me that this inherent ability simply to sit on water, as relaxed as a human being in an easy chair, feet up, smacked of the ridiculous. So I quacked at her. She cocked her head a few more degrees to one side, inquiringly. Encouraged, I continued. 'Quack, quack, quack,' I said.

'Quack,' she replied, monosyllabic. But it was a funny sort of quack; a quack that wasn't quite a quack.

'Are you really a duck?' I said. 'You look like a duck, but you do have a right queer quack.' She declined to commit herself further.

The phone on my desk began ringing. 'How's it coming along?' said the magazine editor.

'You're panting,' I said.

'Good god, man, it's a rush job!' he said.

'But I'm the one who's rushing,' I said. 'Why should you be panting?'

'I'm stuck with four empty pages in *my* magazine,' he said.

'Never fear,' I said.

'But will you get the story through in time?'

'It's a pushover,' I said, then added, 'Look, I can't talk now; I'm interviewing a duck.'

'Good man!' he said. 'Go to it!' And he hung up.

I put down the receiver and waited for the phone to ring again. To my surprise, it didn't. In a way, the failure of the editor to ring back worried me. It indicated either (a) that this particular editor considered an interview with a duck a good magazine story, which offended my journalist's instincts or, (b) that the editor hadn't really been listening to what I had been saying, which I had often suspected. Somewhat glumly I considered the typewriter keyboard and, for possibly the ten-thousandth time in my writing career, slowly tapped with one finger the letters on the second top row—QWERTYUIOP.

Qwertyuiop! In itself, an interesting word. I had long had a hankering to fit it into a TV script or a play, perhaps as the name of a country town. The porter at the local railway station would be calling,'Qwerrrrrr-ty-uiop!' With a smartly-clipped final syllable sounding like 'yup' but with infinitely more subtle inflection.

The duck was still swimming around with the seagulls. I quacked at her without enthusiasm, but she merely cocked her head to one side and fixed me with her little eye. So I blew a raspberry at her and again turned to my typewriter. Suddenly businesslike and purposeful, I whipped out the xxxxx-d sheet of paper so that the roller whirred against its ratchet, and I threaded in a new sheet. Then I slapped my cheeks briskly three or four times, partly to stimulate the flow of blood to the brain and partly to let myself know that I was horsing around, and began typing.

I was lounging on the terrace muching a lunchtime salami sandwich, chortling at a water-ski novice teetering in a drunken crouch in the wake of a distant boat and thinking how pleasant it was both to live and to work in this quiet wooded arm of the harbour, when the white Muscovy duck came flying along the shoreline. Charming, I thought, how vastly superior to a plaster duck stuck on a living-room wall. She did a circuit of the bay, long neck outstretched, wings beating rhythmically, then thrust out her yellow-webbed feet, steadied her wings, and glided in for a somewhat wobbly landing. She swam toward me, and I stood up and walked to the railing on the edge of the terrace to examine her more closely. Immediately, she back-pedalled a few metres out into the bay. It was impossible to say whether she was alarmed by my advance or by the fact that I had suddenly grown a body, arms and legs since all she had seen of me so far was my head above the window sill.

As a goodwill gesture I threw her the crust of my sandwich. She swam quickly toward it as a dozen or more seagulls, who had played the game before, rose squawking from the decks of the moored boats on which they perched to the continual annoyance of the owners, and swooped down on the floating piece of bread. But she beat them to it. 'Good for you!' I cried. (I have long had a sort of love–hate relationship with seagulls, which I find beautiful, graceful, quarrelsome, selfish creatures.)

I took another sandwich from the plate, extracted the salami, popped it in my mouth, and held up the bread to let the birds see that I intended throwing it. The seagulls flapped about like a bunch of squabbling kids, pecking spitefully at one another, but the duck just sat there, alert, head cocked, an eye fixed on the slice of bread in my hand. I threw the bread into the water near her, and she thrust herself forward with her wings and broad webbed feet and snatched it up. 'So you're hungry, eh?' I said. To beat a seagull to food on its home ground, a Muscovy duck has to be hungry.

I threw a few more scraps, favouring the duck to the frustration of the seagulls, then, having distributed my largesse, returned to my desk and the uncompleted urgent magazine story. I was working well when I made the mistake of looking out of the window; the duck was still treading water outside and was looking up at me. I found her cricked neck and fixed little eye strangely disquieting, so I drew the curtains.

I was aware, of course, that this negated one of the main reasons for continuing to live on the foreshore of the harbour. But whereas thousands of other waterfront dwellers snatch

up their binoculars every time something of interest appears—
a yacht whose swearing crew is wrestling with a hopelessly
fouled spinnaker, a cruising water-police launch whose offi-
cers are striving to maintain an earnest demeanour as they
soak up the sun—I had found that I was forced to draw the
curtains. I had to: otherwise I'd get nothing done, and a
freelance writer either produces the goods or he's in the poor
house.

I typed another sentence, but it didn't jell. I kept seeing
that hungry little eye. I pulled out the sheet of paper, threw
it in the wastebasket, and tried again. The result was worse.
My thoughts drifted away. . .I wonder what it eats? The local
seagulls do very well dive-bombing shoals of fish, but I'm
sure that if a Muscovy duck used the same tactics it would
hit the water like a sack of potatoes.

My eyes wandered to the gap between the curtains, but I
flicked them away and squinted with a show of concentration
at the abstract pattern printed in blacks, shades of gray, and
tomato-sauce red on the off-white curtain fabric in front of
me. Hours of practice over the months had perfected an ability
quite magically to convert the pattern into different forms
simply by opening or closing my eyelids as though varying
the aperture mechanism of a camera. With my eyelids droop-
ing just a little like a beagle's, I could see a mass attack of
V-jet bombers speeding toward their target; half-closed in a
sinister gangster fashion, they enabled me to see flights of
rockets spurting flame as they streaked through space; as
morning-after slits, head tilted back a little to sharpen the
focus, my eyes transformed the pattern incredibly into a troop
of ballet dancers, all leaping about on one foot, each with a
leg stuck out astern. (I am unsure of the specific choreographic
term for this posture.) Pattern-gazing, my conscience told me,
was not merely frittering away time. I had had some of my
best thoughts while squinting at the curtains, although admittedly the ratio of thoughts to squinting-hours was rather low.

Nothing came of the pattern-gazing. I found myself flicking
through my small store of knowledge of domestic poultry: I
was sure that ducks needed a lot of water to drink, but could

they drink *salt* water? A seagull must swallow a couple of buckets of the Pacific Ocean every day, but what effect would that have on the constitution of a freshwater duck? As I dwelt on the problem my more-sensitive-than-thou nature dreamed up an image of a duck dying of thirst while swimming in the umpteeen billion litres that fill Sydney Harbour.

I pulled back the curtains; our eyes met. I sighed. 'Okay,' I said. 'Just this once. Then you can take off.'

I went into the kitchen, cut several rounds of bread, filled a red plastic bowl with fresh water, and walked down the steps which gave access to the jetty and the new slipway I had built to haul my little sailing boat under the cottage. There was a large slab of sandstone to the left of the cottage: the surface of the rock was fairly flat and was above water on all but the highest tides. I put the plastic bowl down on the rock and after hurling several pieces of driftwood at the seagulls to drive them off, began tossing pieces of bread near the duck to entice it toward me. The following conversation ensued:

'Duck, duck, duck, duck, duck!'

'Quack!'

'Yes, I know you're hungry. Here, have some bread.'

'Quack!'

'You know, you have a funny sort of quack. Are you *sure* you're a duck? Yes, of course you are. What's your name? Dora? Is that it? Dora Duck?'

'Quack!'

'I thought so. Here you are, Dora. Nice bread. Duck, duck, duck, duck, duck.'

'Quack!'

'That's a girl. In you come. Here's some water for you, nice fresh drinking water. Duck, duck, duck, duck, duck—No, you fool! Don't swim away. Look, it's water! *Fresh* water! Come here! I'm not going to eat you.'

The last sentence was intended colloquially: Dora took it literally. She obviously had played this sort of game before. She would come so close but no closer.

'Very well. . .' I said inconclusively, and adding, 'I can't waste all day on a duck,' dropped what was left of the bread on the rock and walked back upstairs to my desk. But it took only a few minutes for my curiosity to get the better of me. I crossed the glassed-in sunroom-cum-verandah and from behind a drawn curtain near the kitchen, peeped down at the rock. Dora was drinking thirstily from the red plastic bowl, wagging her tail as happily as a dog lapping the cat's milk. Then she sensed that I was watching her; she stopped drinking, screwed her neck around, and fixed me with her expressionless eye, which already was beginning to look familiar. When she decided that I wasn't going to leap out of the window with an axe she began drinking again. Then she sat down on the rock alongside the bowl, swivelled her neck 180 degrees, and tucked her beak under a wing as if preparing for a nap in the gentle spring sunshine.

I'm sure it's perfectly clear that my motive in feeding Dora was as uncomplicated as that of Good King Wenceslas when the poor man came in sight gathering winter fuel. 'Bring me flesh, and bring me wine,' sang the King, 'bring me pine logs hither; thou and I will see him dine, when we bear them thither.' That was all he committed himself to. His expressed intention was merely to stand the man a feed. I doubt that the song would ever have been written had Good King Wenceslas looked out of his palace window the day after the Feast of Stephen and seen the poor man once more standing there in the snow with his bundle of sticks and a beady look. A fair thing is a fair thing.

I think that subconsciously I was stuck with the migratory bird idea and had a mental picture of Dora, rested and replete, circling above the cottage and dipping her wings in thanks for a simple act of human kindness before heading arrow-straight for the Antarctic.

I was surprised, therefore, at the end of the day, to hear a scraping sound outside. I put down the manuscript I had been checking and walked across to the window near the kitchen. Dora was waddling around the rock, tail wagging, her beak opening and closing rapidly in the near-empty bowl which she was pushing ahead of her as she tried to drink the last centimetre of water in the bottom.

'What!' I said. 'You're still here.' She glanced up at me, then continued to pursue the bowl around the rock. I watched this performance critically; the answer to her problem was obvious to me, and I couldn't resist giving her advice. 'Put your foot in it,' I said. She stopped perambulating and cocked her head to look up at me. 'Put your foot in it,' I repeated. 'Hold the dish down while you drink.' But the message didn't get through. She wagged her tail several times, hopefully. 'No,' I said. 'I'm not giving you any more; you must have drunk five litres. Finish what you've got, then, if you're heading south, you'd better get started; you've got a long way to go.' She again wagged her tail and sat down beside the bowl. It was quite apparent that she had no intention of flying anywhere—least of all to the Antarctic.

The situation had to be handled with tact but firmness. 'Look,' I said. 'I'm sorry, but I don't want a duck. In fact, I don't want a pet of any kind. I live here on my own, I'm a single man, and I'm extremely busy. I just can't be tied down to feeding schedules and all that sort of thing. Being deputy master to a dingo is quite enough, thank you. Besides, without offence, I'm afraid I have no affinity with poultry. Now beat it.' And I opened the window and flung out an arm to point the way south. Alarmed by the movement she hurled herself off the rock and flew low to the water along the foreshore until she was out of sight, And that, I thought, was that. I went down to the rock and picked up the bowl and went back upstairs to relax with a well-earned drink before dinner. At dusk, I stood up to switch on a light and glanced out through a front window. A seagull was perched on one of the two posts at the end of the jetty; Dora was perched on the other.

Quite suddenly, memory whipped me back to childhood, to something nasty at the bottom of the garden—father's chicken yard.

* * *

I can still smell the hot bran-and-pollard mash and see the steam rising sluggishly in the thick winter-morning air. I can feel the warmth of the old saucepan on the palms of my hands as I trotted across the crackling, frost-white grass, past the vegetable patch, to the chicken pen in the corner of the backyard formed by the three-wired, country town fence. And I can still hear the clucking as the fowls scrambled stupidly to get at the food, and feel the brush of feathers as one rushed past me to escape through the gate, and sense my rage when, driving that one back in, two more darted out. And I can smell the sour, confined-bird smells as I raked the droppings on the ground. And I can also feel water sloshing in my shoes as I spilled the water tins with the resentful carelessness of a boy performing a detested chore.

It is perhaps because of father's chicken yard that up to this time I had not really been a bird man. I don't mean that I didn't *like* birds. I did. But I preferred to watch them flying around singing their heads off. I was most strongly reminded that I was not a bird man when, as a youth, I had a series of twelve test injections to determine which allergy was causing my hay fever. It turned out that I was allergic to all twelve, but I reacted so violently to the injection containing feathers—don't ask me how they managed to inject feathers—that a scar remained. I couldn't bear to handle father's chickens, and I'd mow the whole lawn or chop half a ton of firewood rather than assist in an execution or even the simple transfer of birds from one pen to another.

At one time, I boarded with two pleasant spinsterish ladies who kept a grey South African gallah, Jacko. For some reason Jacko took a shine to me, and I felt obliged to converse with him and feed him peanuts—not only because the ladies were charming but because they plied me with fine food, washed and ironed my shirts, and restitched buttons while they were still holding by a reasonable thread or two. I'll long remember an excruciating hour spent with Jacko attached to my right forefinger. When Jacko latched on to something he'd only let go when offered something edible as compensation. As he needed one leg to stand on he had to release what he was holding in order to take what was being offered.

On this occasion I thoughtlessly wagged a finger at him through the bars of his cage in passing. At least, I thought I was passing. Jacko promptly grabbed the finger with his left claw and hung on; and he continued to hang on, despite cajoling, pleas, curses, and the wagging of other fingers as bait, while he solemnly recited to me, his captive audience, his entire remarkably extensive repertoire from 'Jacko wants a cup of tea' to 'One, two, three, four six—damn it all, I forgot the five.'

A traumatic experience. Added to my childhood years of servitude in father's chicken yard and my feather allergy, it reinforced my indifference to birdlife other than free and on the wing.

At nine o'clock, Dora was still on the jetty post, alert, head cocked to one side. She had been staring up at the house for hours. Unnerving tactics. In the end, I again sighed and muttered, 'Okay, just this once. . .' I filled the plastic bowl with water and looked around for something in which to mix a bread mash. The most suitable receptacle seemed to be a small chrome-plated tray.

I carried the bowl and tray downstairs in the dark and put them on the rock, being careful not even to look toward Dora, who was still perched on the post. My intention was to create the impression that anything she might find was pure chance, that the local food supply was extremely uncertain, and that she'd be far better off somewhere else.

I was no sooner back inside the house than I heard the flap of her wings, a splash, then a 'skliffing' sound, presumably made by the tray scraping against the rock.

I peered through a gap in the curtains. Dora showed as a patch of white on the rock beside the plastic bowl and chrome-plated tray. It was apparent that she found little fault with an establishment which served a duck its dinner on a silver salver.

5

'I see you've got a duck'

You were wrong, I said to myself, to feed her in the first place. If you hadn't someone else would have. I know that's the sort of statement that starts you complaining that that's what's wrong with the world: everybody leaves everything to everybody else. But, in this instance, I am sure it's safe to say that somebody else *would* have fed her. Anyway, how do you know that she doesn't belong to someone? She's obviously a domestic duck. You've probably committed alienation of affections.

I was behind drawn curtains as though pinned down by enemy sniper fire, not daring even to take a peep outside. I believed I knew what I would see in the morning light—Dora perched on the jetty post, head cocked to one side, her eye fixed on mine, saying matter-of-factly, without apology, 'I know you've got a loaf of bread up there, share it.'

The sheet of paper in my typewriter was blank; patterned flights of ducks were winging all over the curtains. It looked like being a lousy day. I began thinking about getting a job as a builder's labourer, or buying a delicatessen, or joining the diplomatic service. Pondering on these alternatives, each of which at that moment had its own particular appeal, I risked a squint through the curtains. To my surprise and relief Dora was not on the jetty post; she was in the middle of a flock of seagulls scratching around on the sandflat at the end of the bay to the right of the cottage. I congratulated myself on having got rid of her and chided myself for getting upset about the ridiculous notion that I had become responsible for the welfare of a Muscovy duck. It was apparent that the creature was quite capable of caring for herself and had acquired a taste for seafood.

I watched the birds for some time, finding them an interesting study in contrasts; the seagulls dancing lightly on their dainty red feet, Dora waddling heavily on her broad yellow webs; the gulls pecking at specific delicacies, Dora shovelling with her beak, using much the same technique as a front-end loader.

Then the seagulls flew off, squawking, to investigate a patch of broken water in the centre of the bay, but Dora didn't follow. She launched herself and began paddling toward the cottage. Quickly, I drew back from the window and began typing very briskly, 'Yankee Doodle went to town riding on a pony while the quick brown fox jumped over the lazy dog and all good men came to the aid of the party crying the evil that men do lives after them the good is oft interred with their bones. . .' which is a trick I use to get the wheels working. If I'm in luck I keep going and type something useful. It worked; I did.

Around lunchtime, Larry Cole, the tenant in the Muirs' cottage, looked in through the open door. He and his wife Vera were splendid neighbours. At that time, I was again flat out with a series of writing projects and they were appalled by the concept of someone working all hours of the day and night seven days a week. Repeatedly at weekends, I would be all but physically hauled from my desk to share a barbecue and a glass of red wine. Larry enjoyed his glass of red. He was bush born and bred but after a night out with the boys, which occurred at not infrequent intervals, his bushmanship and sense of direction went astray and the still night would be shattered as he roared to his wife for help, having somehow strayed from the path and ended up in a patch of scrub further along the bay.

'I see you've got a duck,' Larry said, his large frame in the doorway.

'Eh?' I said. I was still deep in the world of my story. Slowly I emerged. 'Oh, you mean Dora. No, she's not mine. She seems to be a stray; I've simply given her a handout.'

'A stray duck? Is that so? I don't believe I've ever heard of a stray duck.' He came inside and together we crossed to the kitchen window to look down at Dora, who was standing on one leg beside the plastic bowl and chrome-plated tray, head tucked under a wing, one eye showing. 'Umm,' Larry rumbled, perhaps subconsciously patting his girth. 'A stray, you say. Looks like a pure Muscovy.'

'Do you think so? I thought she was.'

'No doubt about it. A fine duck. Don't you want her?'

'I haven't got her. In fact, I wish she'd fly off.'

'You do? They're good table birds, you know, Muscovies. Well marinated we could try her on the barbie.'

Suddenly I became protective. 'Sorry, Neighbour Cole, duck's off. Try the sausages and three veg.' And added, 'Anyway, you'd never catch her.'

He grinned, rather slyly, I thought. 'Someone might shoot her.'

'Shooting's against the law in suburbia. I'd have to report them, whoever they were.'

'Oh! Then why don't you cage her? Duck eggs are delicious.'

'I can't bear to see birds caged.'

Larry shook his head. 'Then I guess the sharks will get her. Seems a dreadful waste.' And he wandered out.

I stood at the window considering Dora for a while. It was becoming increasingly obvious that she wasn't going to be around for very long anyway. Her future seemed to have several alternative courses, each of which led to a violent end. Sydney's Middle Harbour is notoriously shark infested; notices along the foreshore warn swimmers against entering the water, and the chances were that Dora would soon disappear in one gulp. (Actually, I have only ever seen one shark in Middle Harbour, but I accept its reputation without quibble. There have been three fatalities that I know of within a few kilometres of the cottage.) The local human population seemed as potentially dangerous to Dora as the sharks. I became aware that basically there are two types of people: those who look at a Muscovy duck and see it as a living creature, all white feathers and big yellow feet; and those who see it as something crisp and golden brown on its back on a plate, drumsticks in the air.

Dora's cold eye looked up at me saying clearly, 'Come on! It's noon. Where's the bread mash?'

I weakened. 'Very well,' I said. 'If you're destined for a short life, I suppose the least I can do is provide occasional supplementary rations.' Then I felt the need to cover myself. 'But don't take it for granted. In fact, the sooner you hop it the better. And keep a lookout for shark fins.'

Weeks passed by, and to my surprise Dora continued to survive. As soon as I got out of bed each morning I went to the front window to look for her. Sometimes she was standing on the rock; more often she was foraging on the sandflat at the end of the bay, waddling among the seagulls. On the mornings when I couldn't see her anywhere I felt an odd mixture of relief that perhaps she had flown off at last, and concern that she might have been swallowed by a shark or ended up as someone's dinner. But by the time I was having breakfast, she would either come paddling along the foreshore or would fly into the bay, circle the boats on the moorings, and glide in for a landing in front of the cottage.

I could never watch her landing without a feeling of apprehension, each time expecting to see her disappear straight into a shark's maw. But as Dora couldn't read the warning notices on the foreshore that said DANGER. . .MAN-EATING SHARKS. . .KEEP OUT OF WATER, she seemed unaware of the existence of sharks and regarded the harbour as her safety zone. Whenever she sensed danger on land, she took to the water with surprising speed. At night, she slept either on the edge of the rock or on a jetty post. To escape from dogs, cats, giant bush rats and human beings, she had only to fall off the rock or the post. She was vigilant 24 hours a day.

Walter, the elderly father of my landlord, was still painting the outside of the cottage, working on scaffolding that had been erected out over the water. He was making steady progress doing just a little every now and then in deference to his 78 years. Walter would look down from the walkway at Dora swimming below and recite with a chuckle, 'Peas, parsnips, potatoes,' and she would look up at him suspiciously as though she recognised the inference and knew that Walter was only half joking.

In time, I found a certain monotony in tearing apart slices of bread morning and evening and mashing them with water, and I began pondering the question of a duck's diet. If I found it monotonous, how did Dora feel about it? She had to eat it. I had noticed that in her excursions around the bay she spent hours swimming around the moored boats pecking at the weed which grew on the hulls and on the mooring chains. This stirred my memory, and I heard my father saying, 'They've got to have green feed. If you want results they've just got to have green feed'. And I recalled that our fowls were let out regularly to graze on the back lawn.

My solution to the green feed problem wasn't quite so simple: my lawned terraces were at the top of a steep cliff five metres above the surface of the harbour, and ducks, like seaplanes, are designed for landing on water. So grazing was out. Late one afternoon, trusting that I was unobserved by my neighbours and reassuring myself that my actions were prompted by scientific interest, I tore a few handfuls of grass out of the lawn, took them inside, and cut the grass up finely with a pair of scissors. I then presented the chopped grass to Dora as a side salad with the bread mash on the silver salver. She scoffed the grass before she touched the bread.

After indulging in a little self-flattery at my perceptiveness, I considered varying her diet even further and found a local store that stocked poultry food. The alternatives were wheat or laying pellets. Which to buy? I believed Dora was a duck (female), but what if she were in fact a he? What effect did laying pellets have on a drake? The young man in the store—a salesman who probably had never even seen a live duck—was unsure, although he fancied it unlikely that the bird would explode. I decided that it would be best to get expert opinion once and for all on what ducks ate, how much and when. I rang the State Department of Agriculture.

'The Duck Department, please,' I said.

'The what?'

'The. . .I would like to speak to an expert on ducks.'

'Oh,' said the voice. 'I'll put you through to Poultry.'

A male voice said, 'Hello.'

'I want to make an inquiry about the feeding of Muscovy ducks,' I said. 'Are you an expert in this field?'

'I probably can help you. What's your particular problem?'

'I want to know what they eat, how much and how often.'

'I gather you're a newcomer to duck raising.'

'You could say that.'

'Well, the nutritive requirement of adult ducks is similar to that of hens. You should supplement the breeding ration with riboflavin in the same way as for breeding hens to ensure adequate hatchability.'

'I see.'

'Here's a summary of the nutritional requirements of breeding ducks: 15 per cent protein, 2.5 per cent calcium, 0.8 per cent phosphorous, 40 parts per million of manganese. . .'

It was time to interrupt. 'Er, excuse me. . .'

'Yes?'

'I'm sorry, but I feel rather like a new mother at the clinic. Could you be a little less technical? What do they actually *eat* and how much?'

'Wet feed or dry?'

Dora seemed happy with the soppy bread mash: I took a stab. 'Wet.'

'Right. Take this down. In the old measure, wheatmeal 20½ pounds, pollard 40 pounds, bran 30 pounds, meatmeal 5 pounds, livermeat 4 pounds, salt ½ pound. That makes up 100 pounds of feed.'

'Oh,' I said. There was quite a long pause.

'Did you get it down?' he said.

'Yes, but. . .can you cut back on those proportions a bit?'

'All right. To what, for instance?'

I had nothing to lose. 'How much do I need for one?'

'One?'

'Yes, one. You see, I have this duck. . .'

'Oh, you're fattening it for Christmas.'

Rather indignantly. 'Certainly not.'

'Now I understand. It's a pet.'

'No, it's not a pet.' I wanted to make my relationship with Dora perfectly clear. 'It simply, well, simply dropped in for a while. You see, I live beside the harbour, and this duck was swimming off my jetty, and—well, I can't see the damned thing starve.'

The duck expert laughed. 'It won't do that. If you want to, you can give it, say, three handfuls of bread or wheat morning and afternoon and some grass every now and then. I'll tell you what I'll do. I'll send you our booklet on duck raising.' And he added, 'Good luck.'

The booklet, titled simply *Duck Raising*, duly arrived in the mail. It was certainly packed with information, but its basic purpose ran contrary to mine. It told the reader how to keep a duck alive and well so that sooner or later you could garotte it; I just wanted to keep Dora alive. I skipped through the offensive sections on broiler growing, marketability, prices offered per pound live-weight, and so on, and noted to my surprise that the Muscovy, a native of South America, was not a true duck—which accounted for Dora's lack of a true quack. Deputy master to a dog that couldn't bark I was now occasional provider to a duck that couldn't quack. Intrigued, I read on and came across a section headed Water for Swimming.

'A good pond,' I read, 'is an advantage, particularly for breeding stock. . .to permit immersion of the birds' heads. This is necessary to allow cleaning and to prevent blockage of the nasal passages. . .'

No duck, I thought, has ever had it so good. Dora had all Sydney Harbour to immerse her head in.

Reading further, I came to a section headed Diseases. 'Sinusitis,' I read, 'affects adult ducks and resembles the condition of sinusitis in turkeys. . .'

I'll be hanged, I thought, sinusitis. Along with my hay fever I've been plagued with occasional bouts of sinusitis for years.

Immediately, I felt a sympathy response toward Dora. I picked up the booklet and crossed to the kitchen window to make a spot check for symptoms.

'In the initial stages affected birds shake their heads violently. . .'

Dora was standing on one leg beside the plastic bowl and silver salver, rock steady. No trouble there.

'One or both sinuses may be involved, and the swelling may be so great as to close the eye, leading to impairment of vision. . .'

Dora looked up at me. Her little eye was clear and sharp. There was no question of impairment of vision.

'It appears that a vitamin deficiency or lack of sand, ashes, or shell grit favour the occurrence of this disease, as also does lack of facilities for the birds to clean themselves in sufficiently deep water containers. . .'

Dora, it seemed, had nothing to worry about so far as her sinuses were concerned. She now had a balanced diet, sand and shell grit by the tonne, and several billion litres of water.

6

Enter, the Seven Dwarfs

I snapped wide awake the way I always do. I'm like that, and I realise it can be very depressing to others crawling out of the smog of sleep. No half-world for me. I'm either conscious or un-. My eyes snap open like the starter's gate at a racetrack and I'm off.

I had definitely heard footsteps, footsteps steadily approaching. I lay still and listened. Again, a footstep, tentative, but definitely a footstep. . .a second footstep. . .a third. . .

Rummy! I need you! I suppose you're snoring your head off in Jock's workroom. If I whistle, will you turn the doorknob and come running?

My right hand was on Red Alert ready to grab the donger I keep beside my bed as I lay considering the optional forms of violence masked as self-defence I had at my disposal.

Option 1: Sneak out from between the sheets, donger in hand, lurk behind the doorway. . .*whack!*

Option 2: A sudden leap out of bed screaming '*Aaaaah!*', landing bent-kneed, pigeon-toed, hands raised 'on guard' ready to punch, push, chop, kick—all those things I had half-wrecked myself endeavouring to master in my wing chun kung fu classes on Monday nights.

I settled for the wing chun and had a trial run at putting my hands 'on guard', but in my recumbent position between the sheets I had a distinct impression that my hands had somehow adopted the posture usually assumed for prayer.

What if he had a knife?

I reached for the donger.

The footsteps came closer, now a steady deliberate tread. I couldn't determine where they were coming from. Closer, closer. . .

And passed above my head.

Huh? The cottage was single storey.

Who was in the ceiling, one of Snow White's Seven Dwarfs?

The footsteps reached the outer wall, began returning, treading more heavily, confidently.

Was it Grumpy in little hob-nailed boots? No, it sounds as though there's more than one. Is it Grumpy, Dopey, Sneezy and Doc?

I was half expecting a chorus of 'Hi ho, hi ho, as off to work we go. . .' when the footsteps suddenly became a Bavarian—or wherever Snow White hailed from—folk dance with the dwarfs stomping their feet, slapping their little leather breeches. Then they seemed to form a Rugby scrum and one got away from the pack, rushing across the ceiling.

I dropped the donger to the floor and groaned. Squire Wilcox, you had assured me they couldn't get in! The place was possum-proof you said.

'Is that you, Nibbles?' I called to the ceiling. 'If it is, you're wasting your time. I seldom buy apples and I'm out of lettuce. Go back to the Muirs: their fridge is jammed with the stuff.'

But I knew the possum wasn't going anywhere. Once a brushtail moves into a ceiling it hangs on in there like an earringed skinhead in a London squat.

The Rugby game ended and I lay with eyes rolling at the ceiling, hoping the game hadn't simply stopped for oranges and cool drinks at half time, trying to determine where the possum was settling down for the next fifteen hours or so, marvelling at the way a creature the size of a new-born baby could sound in turn like a sneaky burglar, a workshop full of dwarfs and a football team.

Then from along the bay came a roar, '*V-e-r-a!*' Larry Cole had missed the path again after a session at the club and had drifted off into the scrub.

The response from the neighbouring cottage was only marginally softer. '*Where are you, you bloody fool?*' I had developed a considerable liking for generous, open-hearted Larry, but as one bloke to another. Had I been born female, and fate quirkily decreed that I be Mrs Cole, I would have taken to him with a rolling pin.

'*I'm here!*' roared Larry.

'*Where the hell is here?*' roared Vera.

'*Here!*' roared Larry. '*Ahhhh! Bugger it! I'm in the lantana again!*'

'*Then get out of it!*'

'*I can't see! It's pitch dark! Jeeze, I'm being scratched to death.*'

'*Haven't you got your torch?*'

Silence. I speculated that said torch was either still in Larry's car or had been dropped somewhere along the path.

Then from the cottage. 'Ohhhh!' With exasperation. 'Hang on. I'll come and get you.' And a door crashed open.

Tap, tap, tap.

From overhead.

Oh no! It's found a toy! And Larry thinks he's got problems.

Tap, tap, tap, tap.

That fool of a builder left an offcut of 4x2 in the ceiling fifty years ago. Didn't he know anything about possums?

Tappity tap. . .tap tap. . .tappitty tippitty tap. . .

This could go on and on until the delightful little creature with its big innocent eyes finally gave a yawn and a belch, farted and curled up with its fluffy black tail wrapped around its little pink nose to sleep through the rest of the night and the following day until sunset.

And I remembered Tony and Liz who were nearly driven out of their minds by a possum that made a playpen in the ceiling above their bedroom and equipped it with a baby's rattle. Or that was what it sounded like.

At two, three or four in the morning, submerged in delicious deep sleep, they would hear, rattle, rattle. . .rattle, rattle, rattle. . .

Several times Tony clambered up through the trapdoor in the ceiling but could find nothing. It was a mystery just where the possum had tucked itself away and what was making the noise. Then one night, in the light of a torch, he saw a slim brown tube. It was a medicine bottle half-full of pills that somehow had found its way into the ceiling, possibly carried there by the possum.

Tippitty tap. . .

'Stop leaning on me,' snapped Vera from near the Cole cottage. 'I can't *carry* you, you great lunk.'

Tap, tap, tap. . .

'I'm *not* leaning on ya.' Larry, deeply aggrieved. 'I was jus' patting ya shoulder, saying thanks.'

'Keep your thanks.'

Tappitty tippitty tap. . .

'*Belt up!*' I roared at the ceiling.

'Sorry, mate.' From Larry in almost muffled tones. 'Shhh!' Clearly aimed at Vera.

Oh my gawd! Clapping a hand over my mouth. Larry thought I'd roared at him. 'No, you're okay, Larry!' I called. 'I was yelling at a possum in the ceiling.'

'Possum? What? A bloody possum?. . .Ya want a hand, mate?'

'Are you coming to bed?' The voice of a woman who'd had enough.

'M'ol' mate needs a hand. Coming mate!'

'*L-a-r-r-y!*'

But Larry was on his way along the path between the two cottages.

'Then you can sleep with *him*!' And a door slammed.

I was at my door by the time Larry had thumped it. A watermelon grin; business suit a job for the dry cleaner, sprigs of lantana attached to the cloth; more lantana sprigs in his thick curly hair. 'Where is it, mate?'

A rush of feet across the ceiling.

'Beauty! He's away with the ball! It's a try!. . .No! I'll stop 'im!' Larry clenched his fists and charged in like an over-weight winger following the track of the possum. At the living-room door he did some nifty footwork to negotiate a sharp left, collided with the long sofa and fell on it, laughing. 'The little bugger's tackled *me*!'

A repeat performance of the Bavarian folk dance, stomping of feet, slapping of breeches.

Larry lay back on the sofa looking up at the ceiling, eyes following the path of the possum as it finished the dance, walked to the back of the cottage. 'They can drive ya balmy, ya know.' A long pause. I leaned resignedly against the door jamb, also looking up. 'Drove me so bloody mad one night I took a pot shot with m' .22. Straight through the ceiling. Cost the price of a good dinner to patch the hole, replace the tiles.'

'You missed the possum?'

'Course I bloody missed. Against the law to shoot a possum. Except in Tasmania. . .But they shot millions ya know, years back. Millions!. . .Used to spotlight them m'self as a kid for pocket money. . .Big business. Fur went all over the world. . . A beaut fur. They sold it as everything, *called* it everything—Adelaide chinchilla, beaver, even skunk.' His voice was fading. 'A beaut fur.'

'I'll get you a blanket.'

'Don' bother, mate. I'll be right.' Larry was snoring by the time I returned from the bedroom. I took off his shoes, lifted his feet on to the sofa, put a pillow under his head and covered him with the blanket.

A possum fart echoed around the rafters.

I went back to bed and lay looking up at the blackness. Silence above. Then the steady rhythm of Larry's snoring began reverberating around the living room. My heart went out to Vera. It was going to be a long night.

'It's not Nibbles,' said Jock without looking up from the microscope in his darkroom. Well, he called it a darkroom, but it was actually a section of the hallway of the old house that he'd blocked off, at the same time covering the glass in the front door with black cloth and cardboard. Disconcerting for anyone wanting to make a grand entrance—or a quick exit. He raised his right hand and crooked a little finger. 'Have a look at this.' Jock pushed his chair to one side and I leaned over the workbench to peer through the eyepiece. 'A beautiful inclusion. Couldn't mistake it.'

'It looks like the San Andreas Fault,' I said critically, staring at the broken line that cut across the white light of the diamond. 'Interesting. But does it mean the diamond's not worth much?'

Jock leaned back in his chair, hitched his braces, lit a cigarette, drew deeply. 'Not at all. There's no such thing as a perfect natural diamond, or any gemstone for that matter. Inclusions—you could call them flaws—give a stone its individuality. No two are alike. Mix that diamond up with a hundred others and I'd pick it out. It's as distinctive as a human fingerprint.' I knew this had become his great interest, the identification of gemstones; he was building a name as a respected authority. Jock put the cigarette on the edge of an already-full ashtray and turned back to the microscope. 'Nibbles is in his usual spot. You can check if you like, and put on the kettle for a cuppa while you're there.'

Sure enough a black-tipped grey tail was hanging through the gouged hole in the kitchen ceiling. After my ghastly disturbed night I was tempted to give it a hefty tug. The tail was only half a metre above my head as I moved around the kitchen, filled the electric jug, got out the cups. 'Tea's up!' I called when the jug had boiled and Jock came through to the adjoining dining area and sat at the table. 'Bloody possums,' I muttered. 'I didn't get back to sleep until after two.'

'Phalangers,' said Jock.

'What?'

'Captain Cook got it wrong in 1770. He compared a ringtail phalanger with the American opossum which he was familiar with when making charts for General Wolf in Canada. Brushtails are members of the family Phalangeridae.'

'Oh?'

'None of Australia's 24 species of so-called possums are in

LVINATOR

fact opossums. Cook was a great navigator, but a sloppy speller. He dropped the "o" in the entry in his log and we're stuck with it.' He looked up at the tail dangling through the hole in the ceiling. 'Specifically, Nibbles is a *Trichosurus vulpecula vulpecula*, so named because his long ears, pointed snout and bushy tail are suggestive of a fox, *Vulpes vulpes*.'

I grunted, thinking of the possum shuffling, galloping and playing fiddlesticks in my ceiling while Larry snored what remained of the night away on the living-room sofa.

'Doesn't it drive you balmy up there?' I asked, echoing Larry.

'Nibbles? No. The bedrooms are on the other side of the house. We're not troubled at night so long as he can only get into this section of skillion roof. He sleeps all day so he doesn't bother us.'

'He's certainly found himself first-class accommodation. All he has to do for room service is wave a paw. Have you blocked off the rest of the house?'

'Well. . .'

'So they do get into the bedroom ceiling?'

'At the moment, no.'

'You mean that when you shut off one entry point it's only a matter of time before they find another?'

'Well, yes.'

'Umm.' For a moment or two I pondered on my own problem. 'Then it seems that I should scout around, find where the possum's getting in, wait until it goes out for the night, then block the hole. May I borrow your extension ladder.'

'Certainly.' Jock paused, then added, 'If you can't find where it's getting in I'll lend you the trap.' The voice of experience.

I spent half an hour crawling around the roof and peering under the eaves. I couldn't see how a mouse could squeeze its way into the ceiling space let alone a possum or a phalanger or whatever it was. I swopped the extension ladder for Jock's stepladder and his possum trap.

The term 'handyman' might have been coined for Jock. He was trained as an artist not a tradesman, but there were few jobs he wasn't prepared to tackle. He loved 'inventing' and improving on already established concepts. Consequently, many of the devices he knocked together had a Heath Robinson quality about them and the workmanship—surprisingly, because he was a precise man—was often rough. But his gadgetry usually worked.

Jock's possum trap was a long wooden box with sliding doors at either end which operated like a portcullis. The entrance door, which was weighted with a printer's lead block, was held up by a length of fencing wire inserted in a small hole. The wire was connected to another piece of fencing wire which protruded through a slot in the top of the box where it was hinged by a loop through which passed a short piece of, yes, fencing wire nailed across the slot.

In operation, the possum nibbled its way along a trail of small pieces of apple leading to the open door where it saw a delicious chunky piece of apple core threaded on the end of the hinged wire at the far end of the trap. Enter possum. As soon as the apple core was tugged, the straight piece of wire was levered from the hole in the weighted door which dropped shut. Possum trapped unharmed.

So, first catch your possum.

The next step is to release it in its natural habitat as far as is practical from the ceiling where it has set up house. Your ceiling.

Now, the brushtail, I was to learn, is extremely territorial and doesn't take kindly to being whipped away from its home ground and plonked in a strange locality. There are those who say that a possum is no sooner released from the trap than it sniffs the air, gets its bearings, and with the instincts of a homing pigeon starts plodding back along the track. Stories about possums returning to the ceiling of their choice rival the epic journeys of dogs and cats that have crossed mountains, rivers and prairies to return to their family home.

A brother-in-law of mine who has a sheep property on a largish island in Bass Strait claims that he painted the claws of a trapped possum with his wife's nail polish to identify it, then took the possum to the island's rubbish tip where there was no shortage of sustenance, umpteen kilometres away. It was back before breakfast, he says. Well, more or less. He believes possums like the car ride.

One way to ensure a possum doesn't resume residency, it is said, is to take it across a stretch of water. I was to learn that a number of my neighbours always took the possums they trapped in their ceilings to a park on the other side of the harbour. I suspect there was equal traffic back across the bridge in our direction.

Melbourne journalist Keith Dunstan once told a nice tale of how he used to row across the Yarra River to release possums he trapped, until the night he met another boat being rowed in his direction—with a possum trap on the after thwart.

I climbed up Jock's stepladder and wriggled through the

trapdoor into the ceiling, set the trap and laid the trail of small pieces of apple to the open door.

In the wee hours I heard scuffling noises, the sound of footsteps, then a dull clunk. The Great White Hunter had triumphed. After possum had finished eating the apple there was a certain amount of scuffling then philosophically, presumably, the captive settled down to sleep.

The following night I drove to bushland several kilometres away and opened both doors of the trap. Nothing happened. I bent over and shone my torch into the trap. Possum stared at me wide eyed; it seemed to be wedged tightly with no intention of moving. I turned the trap around to face the bush, and gently prodded possum's rump with a stick. For a minute or two it wouldn't budge then suddenly it shot out and raced up the nearest tree where it disappeared in the foliage. It gave no indication that it intended trudging back along the track.

A couple of months later I had another visitor. I'm sure it was possum B because it didn't demonstrate the nimble footwork of possum A. It was a blunderer incapable, in my judgement, of executing the finely tuned hop, heel slap, hop, heel slap, hop of a Bavarian folk dance.

I made a fine-tooth-comb examination of the roof and eaves and discovered a loose-ended board I had missed before that a possum could pull back and squeeze past.

I set up a listening post at dusk and heard the loose board go slap when poss went out for the night. I immediately climbed up and nailed the board fast. Thenceforth, it was clear to local wildlife that the cottage on the foreshore was off limits.

7

Guest accommodation

Sweating in the heat, I nailed the large packing case on its side to a solid baulk of timber which had been fixed at the foot of the cliff behind Dora's rock for some indeterminate reason at some time in the past. Then I nailed a plank to the timber so that it formed a ramp from the rock to the open front of the packing case.

Dora had flown off in a panic as soon as I had appeared with the case; she had been treading water, watching me from a safe distance of twenty metres or so. 'There,' I said to her when I had finished, 'you now have a duck house. Note how the back will protect you from the southerlies, and how this side will give shelter from both westerlies and the sun. And it's above the level of the highest tides.' She looked at me unblinking, and I continued, 'The fact that I have gone to this trouble demonstrates that I have developed a certain affection for you, but don't get the idea that you can move in perma-nently. Please regard it strictly as a guestroom.'

The speed of a duck's reactions in any situation other than that which demands a leap for life is, to say the least, trying. It takes not minutes or hours, but days or weeks to get something into a duck's head. And once something has been absorbed, it takes just as long to get it out again. At this time, I was not fully aware of this and had been attributing Dora's peculiarities to the stresses she had endured before her arrival.

I believed that in circumstances in which the benefits to be gained were obvious, a duck probably was as smart as any creature.

Dora sat in the sun by the ramp all day; the temperature was in the thirties. It was one of those humid summers when frail souls gasp for breath while mould grows on bathroom ceilings and on leather shoes tucked away in wardrobes. I decided to be patient, acknowledging that Dora was a waif unaccustomed to luxury living. I tried projecting certain key words such as 'sun. . .shade. . .house. . .wind. . .shelter. . .' but found myself unable to get through.

Having gone to the trouble of building the duck house, I was determined that Dora should use it; I could think of no reasonable argument against her using it. It seemed to be merely a matter of training. So over the next few days, whenever I felt I needed a break from work, instead of picking up a book or walking on the terrace or practicing minor scales on the fiddle, I would go down to the rock and solemnly march up and down the ramp. Sometimes she flew a short distance, then paddled back to watch me curiously; other times she just flew off. Whenever she returned to the rock she sat down beside the ramp.

Finally, in exasperation, I shouted at her, 'Look stupid! It's *shade* !' and got down on my hands and knees and thrust my head inside the duck house. This showed up a fault in the design: I nearly fell off the baulk of timber which was only twenty centimetres or so wide.

Perhaps this was the reason for her wariness; maybe Dora was shrewder than I thought. I rummaged around, found a largish sheet of waterproof plywood (a boat's floorboard that had washed ashore), and nailed it to the timber so that it formed what might be described as a patio in front of the duck house. On this, I placed her water bowl and silver salver and laid a trail of bread across the rock and up the ramp. She came ashore and ate the bread on the rock; the seagulls swooped down and got the rest.

I refused to give in. For a generally easygoing character, I can get very pigheaded. Once I start something, I like to finish it. So I continued to waste time laying food trails, flapping my arms at seagulls, and peering from behind the kitchen window curtain. It was a stalemate. I continued to put Dora's food on the patio; she put herself back on her seafood-and-salt-water diet. When another bad storm blew up and waves began washing right over the rock, she didn't waddle up the ramp for shelter; she flew on to the *top* of the packing case and perched there playing her drowned-duck role while the wind howled around her.

Then one mild day when there was no sting in the sun and a breeze blew gently over the harbour and it was a joy to be outdoors, I looked down to see Dora sitting contentedly inside the duck house. She gave the impression it had been home for a lifetime.

No duck, I came to learn, is at its best on dry land. To be fully appreciated a duck should be seen in flight with its long neck outstretched, feet neatly tucked up against its body as if moulded into the aerodynamic line, wings beating in steady rhythm. At first, Dora's flights were quite short. She would fly up and down the shoreline, from the rock to the sandflat or the boats on the moorings; occasionally she would do a complete circuit of the bay, but I'm not sure these were flown by design. Her performance in the air somehow lacked self-assurance. Every time she took off, she wore a surprised expression which said clearly, 'Is this really *me* up here?' and when coming in to land she always had the startled look of a novice driver who has forgotten how to stop the car. Once airborne, she seemed afraid of steadying her wings and repeatedly, when I thought she was about to land in front of the cottage, she would start flapping even more vigorously and keep on going around the bay.

The technique of controlling altitude also appeared to have her tricked; she had no difficulty in gaining height but was decidedly unsure of what she should do to lose it. Her lack of mastery of what, after all, should be fundamental to a bird caused me to discard entirely the theory that she was a wild creature migrating hither or thither. A duck that appears winded after a couple of circuits of a small bay is no candidate for a marathon trip to the Antarctic. It was evident that prior to landing on the harbour, her flight experience had been limited to half-a-dozen wing flaps in a fowl run.

But as Dora built up her number of flying hours, both her stamina and standard of control improved. Months went by, and I noticed that she was spending more time in the air and less scratching on the sandflat and swimming around the boats on the moorings. Also, her flights were longer and had an erratic quality about them. She would fly a number of circuits of the bay to gain height, then head in one direction as though searching for something, then change her mind and fly frantically in the opposite direction. I knew the symptoms all too well: here was a basic demonstration of the birds, bees and flowers theme.

One morning, after climbing to a great height, she headed straight across the harbour until she was a faint white speck, then vanished around a headland. I watched the spot for some time, waiting for her to reappear, then concluded, with mixed feelings, that Dora had at last checked out. I wished her luck and settled down to work.

Late in the afternoon there was the familiar rushing sound of wing beats, and soon Dora was back on the duck house patio drinking thirstily from her red plastic bowl. The long flights across the harbour continued; some nights she didn't return. I questioned her closely: 'Where does he live?' 'Is he going to move in here or are you moving out?' and so on. But her cold little eye said clearly that her private life was her own concern.

She was away when a fierce southeasterly gale hit the city. Twenty- to forty-knot winds drove waves up the harbour; rain sheeted down. The violent weather continued for days, and still there was no sign of Dora. No birds flew in the grey-black sky. I began worrying about her; was she under shelter, or clinging to a rock somewhere not daring to move? Was she getting food, or was she growing weak from hunger? Had she been forced down into the water and drowned? Repeatedly, I looked up from my desk and scanned the sky.

On the fourth day of the storm I saw a white dot above the far shore. It appeared to be a bird moving toward me. I looked through my binoculars. It was Dora. She was belting her way across the harbour like a flack-riddled Second World War bomber on a homing run. Sudden gusts in the strong cross-wind would hurl her off course, and she would flap her wings even faster to counter the drift. Knowing her limitations as a flyer, I felt it was inconceivable that she could make the distance. I expected her to be blown downwind until she was dashed against the trees on the steep slope enclosing the northern side of the bay. But slowly she came closer and closer. I found myself shouting, 'Come on, Dora! Come on, old girl!' and flung open a front window and bellowed encouragement as the wind and the rain blew around me and the papers on my desk were scattered. Then she sighted me standing at the open window and headed straight for me.

She was within metres of home, wings beating furiously, when I saw the familiar panic-stricken look in her eye: she was so wound up she couldn't stop. 'Turn, Dora,' I shouted. 'Turn into the wind,' and I pranced in front of the window with my arms outstretched showing her how.

But she still came on.

'My god!' I thought. 'I'm really going to have a plastered duck on the lounge-room wall.' I checked an impulse to slam the window shut; she would have gone straight through the glass.

Then I shouted again. 'Turn, Dora! Cut your motor! Land! You've made it!'

She was within arm's reach when suddenly she swerved sharply to the right, shut off everything, and dropped like a brick. She hit the water, a wave came whoosh, she flapped her wings wildly once more—and she was home on her rock.

8

'Not bloody ants again'

'I would like to know which end I'm addressing,' I said politely. 'Am I talking to your backside or your head?' The spiny anteater said nothing, which was understandable. The only noises a spiny anteater has ever been known to make are soft grinding noises, as though chewing its gums in exasperation at not being able to talk, and snuffles through the nostrils near the end of its long snout which is understandable when you consider how much time it spends with its nose buried in dirt.

'I don't want you to consider this as an interview,' I continued. 'This is strictly informal. It's just that I've never had the opportunity to meet a spiny anteater before when I've had reference books to hand.'

The brown-to-cream spines jutting out from the body quivered a little as the anteater wrapped itself into an even tighter ball as though closing the door on further conversation. But like a vacuum cleaner salesman I had my foot in the door, so to speak, and settled comfortably on the grass alongside the anteater and opened one of the books I had taken from my bookshelves a few minutes before.

From behind me, up the hillside near the Muirs' house, came a mournful dingo howl, not full-throated, more like the trailing-away sound of the bagpipes at the conclusion of a

Scottish lament. This was followed by one sharp, defiant bark from Blackie.

The two dogs were outraged: I had stolen their spiny anteater. At least, that was the way they seemed to view the situation.

I had been working at my desk when I heard excited barks and yelps on the terrace leading to the Dennises' cottage. Finally, I got up and went outside to find Blackie barking and leaping around an object on the grass while Rummy stood calmly analysing the situation and making exploratory jabs with his forepaws at what proved to be the proximity of a spiny anteater's underbelly. He clearly had learned that there was nothing to be gained by jabbing at the spines.

'Anteater,' I said, 'you're dead unlucky wandering through suburbia, out in the open, and running into the one creature, apart from man, that's ever had you for dinner—the dingo. Or, nowadays, do you have to keep a weather eye open for foxes as well? You're lucky I'm at home to rescue you.' Whereupon I grabbed Blackie and Old Untameable by their collars and heaved them across the terrace, behind the cottage, and up the path a little way where I released them and ordered them home. They stood looking back at me and towards the spiny anteater. I grabbed a stick and waved it menacingly. 'Home!' I said loudly. 'Go home!' Slowly, reluctantly, they walked up the hill.

It was very pleasant sitting on the grass in the May sunshine with the spiny anteater curled up beside me. It must have been pleasant for the anteater as well with the autumn sun warming its back. I immediately concluded that the spiny anteater was a most co-operative subject for study. Birds fly off, animals run or hop away, but here was the anteater curled up in a neat ball going nowhere and with no pressing schedule that I could determine. I started turning pages in a leisurely fashion, pleased that my library contained an increasing number of titles that were adding to my sketchy knowledge of Australian wildlife.

'So, I should formally address you as *Tachyglossus aculeatus aculeatus*,' I said to the bit that I thought was most likely the head. 'That's quite a name for a little chap. No wonder you're usually called an echidna: even spiny anteater is more of a mouthful, and the other option, porcupine, is just not right. You're a short-beaked echidna, as distinct from the long-beaked echidna found in New Guinea.

'What! This other authority says you're *not* an echidna, that an echidna is actually a genus of eel.' I looked down at the spiky ball. 'I wonder how that came about. You're certainly nothing like an eel. But nine-tenths of the population of Australia call you echidna. I think I'll play safe and call you spiny anteater which, after all, is what you are.' The echidna/spiny anteater/porcupine still had nothing to say so I continued, 'It says here that your origins just aren't known, that scientists don't see any direct link in the evolutionary development from reptiles to placental mammals, that somehow you've missed the bus.

'Oh! This can't be good for your psyche: they lump you and the platypus together at the absolute bottom of the scale in the lowliest order of mammals, Monotremata. And all because you're a furred animal that still lays eggs. Further, and this is downright cruel, they say that your brain has less learning capacity than other mammals leading to the conclusion that you are an inferior creature.'

No wonder the spiny anteater lay there all curled up with its head in close contemplation of the navel-that-might-have-been had it got its act together and stopped laying eggs.

Even though the conversation was all one way I found the spiny anteater pleasant and relaxing company. It might not be credited with being bright but it had been smart enough to choose a food line for which there is no competition. And one item not in short supply in Australia is ants.

On reflection I wondered if ants could really be considered food. I couldn't imagine anything more ghastly than a diet of ants: ants for breakfast, ants for lunch, ants for dinner, day after day, year after year. If I turn up in the next life as a spiny anteater I can hear myself bellowing—mentally, lacking vocal chords—in protest: 'Not bloody ants again, woman! How about a decent steak?'

Then again, it's unlikely that I'd be complaining to the missus because spiny anteaters are solitary creatures.

Contemplating my new-found friend this seemed understandable. Many creatures in the wild curl up together for warmth and comfort, but spiny anteaters cannot be considered cuddly. I could see little potential for joy for a close twosome.

At which, I got curious about the physical aspects of procreation. Just how do spiny anteaters go about it without inflicting nasty injuries on each other? I thumbed through the reference books. None supplied an answer. All I learned was that the female lays a single, round, soft-shelled egg, seemingly depositing it directly into a temporary pouch made up from folds of skin on the underbelly that it has the capacity to form by muscular control. There the egg lies for fourteen days until the young non-spiny (at this stage) anteater hatches. Although they are mammals, female monotremes have no teats: milk flows from glands in the pouch and there the young spiny anteater stays until its quills start to grow and its wriggling becomes too much for mother to bear. Junior is then left between feeds in a scooped-out burrow while mother goes off to find more ants.

Phase 1 of procreation was coyly skipped.

Nature has devised some odd tricks to overcome physical difficulties in this department. Male snakes, I have been reliably informed, actually have two penises so that they can have a successful mating whether the approach to the female is made from either port or starboard. The unused penis apparently has the capacity to switch off as though it has had a cold shower and passively ignores the proceedings. It probably has the attitude of 'better luck next time' when the male snake sneaks up on the female from the other side.

It appears that despite the seeming difficulties there is no lack of interest on the part of male spiny anteaters: six, I read, have been observed determinedly following a single female. I scribbled myself a note for more research: 'Spiny anteaters: just how *do* they do it?' then looked around in anticipation of seeing an amorous swain peering from beneath the bushes. But it was a little early: mating, one book said, took place in July and August.

After a thorough inspection of the curled-up creature I began to revise my initial thought that the spiny anteater was an ideal subject for study. All I was studying was a pincushion of quills. Through the erect spines I could see the brown fur that provides the spiny anteater with a warm coat. The fur of the Tasmanian species, *Tachyglossus setosus*, which I have never seen, apparently is so long and thick that it obscures the spines which could give a would-be predator a nasty shock.

Hold on. The quills themselves are actually a modified form of hair. Now that's an interesting one. Just as well the development didn't extend to the human species. Wouldn't have done a thing for the codes of football, for instance. Heading a soccer ball would be disaster, and there'd be no joy in packing down in a Rugby scrum. And as for stroking your loved one's golden tresses. . .

While examining the anteater I speculated on where it lived. I knew that spiny anteaters didn't dig burrows but made do with shelter in hollow logs and under rocks, bushes or debris. I had seen an anteater occasionally around the bay, and once on a mown verge a block or so away, but I had no idea how many were in the area. 'Where do you live?' I asked the spiky ball. 'Do you have a home in the bush at the end of the bay or do you simply wander around the hillside like the Flying Dutchman?' It clearly had no intention of satisfying my curiosity. It was staying curled up, secure in the knowledge that sooner or later whatever was bothering it would tire and go away. It was right; I did. But only as part of my strategy: I decided to make the kitchen my observation post.

Washing up a modest accumulation of dishes with a minimum of clatter I was able to maintain a watch on the spiky ball on the terrace through the windows above the sink. The phone rang but I ignored it, concerned that if I got involved in a long conversation the subject of my study would slip away. Having washed the dishes I filled the salt cellar, added peppercorns to the pepper grinder, and topped up the sugar bowl. These little tasks had the dual effect of sparing me from minor irritation next time I sat down for a meal and creating the illusion that my time was being spent profitably.

Still no movement on the terrace.

Putting the salt, pepper and sugar back in the food cupboard I noticed a fine trail of small black ants along one of the shelves headed arrow-straight for a jar of strawberry jam.

A bell rang! I sensed victory in the eternal war I wage with ants along with 99 householders out of 100 right around the country. Cats are kept as mousers; why shouldn't spiny anteaters be kept as anters? I could see a *Tachyglossus aculeatus aculeatus* patrolling the kitchen, ever vigilant, long sticky tongue flashing out like D'Artagnan's rapier the moment a head popped out of one of the cracks in the wall that led to the ant metropolis somewhere in the bowels of the cottage. As a spiny anteater needs untold thousands a day to satisfy its appetite, very soon it would be farewell ants. The concern would be how to supplement the anteater's rations once it was on top of the problem.

Oh for a word with the redoubtable Mrs Edith Coleman.

Mrs Coleman, I had read, kept spiny anteaters in captivity in Melbourne before the Second World War and wrote authoritatively on their behaviour. She found that they adapt readily to domestication and in addition to ants, larvae, and crunched-up wood grubs, slaters and slugs, they enjoy milk and an occasional raw egg which is eaten through a hole in the shell.

I could manage all that. A pet spiny anteater could be quite engaging once it got used to me and unravelled itself. One would need to be wary, of course. No more wandering around the house in the dark in bare feet; vigilance would be needed when flopping down in an easy chair to watch telly.

But think of an ant-free kitchen.

Another problem might be the layout of the furniture—with which I was now quite satisfied. It's on record that a zoologist once locked a spiny anteater in his kitchen for the night. The next morning he found that table and chairs, some boxes, and to cap it, the kitchen dresser, had been moved out from the walls and pushed towards the middle of the room. It's quirky, but it seems that spiny anteaters have a passion for rearranging furniture and they do know their own strength.

There was action on the terrace. Four furry legs and a round, brown, furry face with a long, fine nose, tiny eyes, and a sadsack expression had unravelled from the cluster of spines. The anteater was heading for the scrub on the wooded hillside, totally ignoring my home-grown supply of ants, moving with the rolling gait of a sailor ashore after a long spell at sea.

I slipped out through the kitchen door and stood watching intrigued as it started to climb up the bank: it was using its nose or beak like an alpine mountaineer's ice axe to help haul its body up the steep incline.

After a dozen or so metres it paused, scratched the ground with its forepaws, and prodded the humus with its nose searching for ants or beetle larvae. Apparently, whatever adhered to its long, slim, sticky tongue would be drawn in through the tiny, toothless mouth and mashed between horny pads at the back of the tongue and on the palate.

The anteater moved further up the hill and I followed at a distance. I would dearly have liked to have a chat with the anteater, uncurled, man to man, face to sadsack face. But I knew that at the first approach it would curl up again, tuck in its head, and contemplate the navel that might have been.

When a twig cracked under my weight, a sound so soft I hardly heard it, the anteater slipped into the gap between a rock and the trunk of a tree it had been examining and the spines extended. Locked in there, nothing would move it. I stood quietly, remembering when my Staffordshire bull terrier, Toro, excitedly bailed up an anteater in the Snowy Mountains one summer. His nose bled from a dozen spine pricks.

In five minutes or so the anteater lowered its spines, came out from between the rock and the tree trunk, and continued on its way.

Then ahead and to my left I saw a shape under a thick bush. Rummy was looking intently at the anteater. I wondered how long he had been in the scrub on the hillside, watching the anteater, watching me. He moved a step or two, quickly, silently.

'No, Rummy!' I said sharply.

But a dingo on the hunt takes orders from no one. Ignoring me, Rummy bounded forward. As he did so the anteater's spines extended, there was a flurry of movement as claws dug furiously in the soft earth, and while Rummy's paws dabbed at the air above its spines the anteater sank into the ground as a submarine sinks beneath the waves.

9

All that glitters. . .

'It's clearly genuine,' said Jock. He had pushed aside a collection of rock samples to clear a space on one of several tables that contributed greatly to the congestion in his workroom. More samples were piled in boxes under the tables and stacked against the walls. More still were being washed in a sink in a corner of the room which originally had been an open verandah with a wood-burning stove that had once served as a kitchen, a common practice in old Australian houses.

Then there were gem cutters and grinders and polishers, several spare electric motors taken from washing machines, lawnmowers and who knows what that just might come in handy one day, miners' picks, geologists' hammers, sieves. . .

Even the back wall was rock, a handsome sandstone wall supporting the terrace behind the house that Jock had utilised to enclose the room. He was proud that it remained bone dry in the heaviest downpour and would draw a finger over the film of dust thrown out by the cutters, grinders and polishers to prove it.

The impression would have been of being in a storeroom on a mine site but for a glass wall and tall double glass doors that opened on to a courtyard shaded by a magnificent wisteria vine and, inside, a range of unrelated objects that included the skull of a steer, a cluster of bows and arrows from the New Guinea highlands, several non-matching oars that had been washed ashore over the years, and a partly dissembled, possibly never-to-go-again, outboard motor most kindly described as a vintage model.

Rummy lay on his rug where he had a view of the court-yard. It was his room as well.

I peered across rocks at the upside-down sheet of paper torn from a notebook that Jock had laid in the cleared space, then wormed my way between two tables to get a better, right-way-up view.

I grinned at him. 'Someone's pulling your leg,' I said. 'A kid's drawn it.'

He drew on his cigarette then said in his deliberate way, 'Not at all. The printing is too well formed for a child. I would say the map has been drawn by someone not particularly well educated. Which would be understandable.'

'But it's a pirate treasure map. I used to draw them as a boy; just like that, with the tantalising words, "Gold buried here".' And I jabbed a finger at the cross on the sheet of paper.

Jock lit a fresh cigarette from the butt of the other which he stubbed out on a lump of rock. He looked up at me over the top of his glasses, a thumb hooked under his braces. His expression clearly indicated that he was in possession of superior knowledge. 'But there is no word "buried", and "here" is a gully running up from the Turon River. Thousands of ounces of gold were taken out of the Turon from the 1850s on.'

I looked down at a double line that squiggled across the page. 'How do you know it represents the Turon River?'

It was his turn to jab a finger, at a letter 'S' which was on the western edge of the map. 'Sofala is on the Turon. It was the main town in the early days. And I've compared the map with an official Ordnance map. It's crude, but it matches the topographical features.' Jock drew on the cigarette; I sensed a punchline coming. 'And I found it in a book on the gold rushes I was looking up at the mining museum. Someone will be kicking himself; he was silly enough to use it as a book-mark—for the chapter on the Turon.'

'So, are you getting a miner's licence, abandoning Jean and the kids and heading west?'

'I've already got a miner's licence, and it's scarcely west. The Turon is north of Bathurst, just over the range a few hours drive away. I was thinking we could go for the long weekend.'

'We?'

'Yes, just the two of us.' Rather secretively, as to a man you could trust. I could see the pricking of thumbs and a blood oath coming up. 'We could leave after lunch on the Friday.'

'Jock, remember the times we've been fishing, sitting in the boat for hours on end, all to no avail.' He had no option but to nod. 'Probably the fish were there somewhere, but there was all that water around them. It's the same with gold. But gold is surrounded by dirt, tonnes and tonnes of dirt. At least, with fishing you just sit; with gold, you dig.'

'That's the excitement of it.' And I could see Jock in moleskins and check shirt, tent and swag on a creek bank, digging and gold panning his way from Ballarat to the Palmer River. Jock had been born in the wrong century.

'So you won't come?' He knew damn well it didn't take much to persuade me to go bush.

'As chief cook and bottlewasher, tent erecter, even hewer of wood and drawer of water, yes. But when it comes to digging, you're on your own. I concede all the profits are yours.'

Jock shook his head slowly. He couldn't believe that anyone could find swinging a pick hour after hour unappealing. Just as well he wasn't a punter; he had no concept of odds.

'Jock, do you really need all this?' One didn't have to be a Fulbright scholar to see that there was pretty well two of everything—picks, shovels, crowbars, etc. etc. etc., all items associated with hard labour—filling the back of his station wagon. 'You do remember the deal? I'm chief cook and bottlewasher, tent erecter, hewer of wood and drawer of water?'

'Yes, yes,' he said tetchily. 'You can't have too many tools.' He was dressed in his standard rig for a fossicking expedition, big boots, old army slouch hat, baggy shorts of a cut known as 'Bombay bloomers', and a safari jacket. Somehow, he seemed to smack of the African veldt or India's Punjab, rather than the Australian bush. I understood his fondness of the safari jacket; it was largely comprised of pockets, and every one was bulging.

Not a dull trip marked by prolonged periods of silence. Jock drove. We discussed the formation of the clouds that were overhead, Jock declaring that they were not the type of cloud that produced rain, and this spun off to the development of cyclones. That led to the value of the space program in weather forecasting. We then had a hearty difference of opinion over the order of Henry VIII's six wives, before stopping for intermission over a couple of beers at a country pub. After that, we got on to folk music, possibly because Slim Dusty had been singing on the radio in the bar, the origins of folk music, of which I confess my knowledge is slight.

However, I was able to recount my joy on unexpectedly stumbling across the Cornish village of Helston on Flora Day, the day of the annual Furry Dance. Yes, Furry Dance, don't ask me why. After describing how the village band 'with a curious tone of the cornet, clarinet and big trombone. . .' really did weave up and down and around the town and in and out of all the houses—playing with a surprisingly dirge-like tempo—I sang the chorus and all three verses of the song based on the tune made popular by good old Peter Dawson, and a superb voice he had.

To my surprise, because he was anything but a vulgar man, Jock responded with the bawdy Celtic ballad—if such it can be called—'The Ball of Kerrymore', a performance which, I concede, was of epic proportions. With impeccable timing he was finishing what seemed to be the twentieth verse of the remarkable goings on that night at Kerrymore as we rolled down the hill into what was left of Sofala in the Turon Valley and pulled up in front of the pub.

Not much was left of the old rip-roaring gold town,

although in more recent years it has been tarted up to attract the tourist trade. At this time, it was tumbledown and raw, extremely raw. However, the sole remaining pub still had character—and characters—and we walked through the door straight into one.

It wasn't a matter of heading for another corner of the bar; it's not all that big, and the character was the only customer. He was six foot three if he was an inch, dressed in well-soiled black shirt and riding pants, with riding boots and a stockman's hat. His eyes were bloodshot from a week on the booze, his left cheekbone was bruised. I'd met him, that is, his counterparts, a dozen times before. He was trouble.

I don't believe Jock even noticed him; after the twenty or whatever verses of 'The Ball of Kerrymore' he was intent on a drink. He breasted the bar right alongside the character and slapped down a note.

The stockman lurched back a step to get Jock in focus, and looked him up and down. I looked around for a high stool, not with the idea of sitting on it.

'Two beers,' said Jock.

The stockman was taking in the Bombay bloomers and the safari jacket. Then suddenly he roared, 'A bloody *pom*!'

Jock drew his wiry frame to its full height of five foot seven, tilted his head back to meet the stockman's eyes and said calmly in a broad brogue he only occasionally affected, 'Och! I'm a *Scot*, mon.' And to the barman with a grin, 'You'd better make that three beers the noo, laddie.'

'It's up to you,' the barman murmured, clearly happy to be on his side of the bar.

'Umm!' the stockman grunted, stuck for a word. 'Can't stand bloody poms.'

'M' forebears used to take their cattle,' said Jock.

'What? Were they bloody duffers?'

'Not a bit,' said Jock. 'They reckoned they were simply taking back what the Sassenachs had taken from them.'

'Beauty!' declared the stockman approvingly. 'Bloody beauty! Have a drink.'

'I've already bought you one,' said Jock, and pushed the third glass toward him.

So Jock bought him a drink. Then he bought us a drink. Then I bought us a drink. I'd been this way all too many times before in bush pubs. I think of it as the 'shouting merry-go-round' and it's not an easy one to step off while the music's playing. A shout received must be reciprocated with a shout given. There are no rules for ending it. And all the time I could see the stockman's mood swinging like a pendulum; what he was getting was friendliness when what he really wanted was a good fight.

If Jock was aware of this he didn't show it. He questioned him about his work as a stockman with genuine interest; not the personal side of his life, just his work. He wasn't a local; he was from 'out west' and claimed to be a ringer, a number one stockman. Who knows what he was doing in Sofala; I couldn't see him swinging a pick.

Then Jock said, 'Before we go, let me buy you just one more drink—and may I have a look at your ring?'

'Huh?' The big man looked down at his right hand; a large gold ring set with what appeared to be a huge ruby was on the little finger. He looked suspiciously at Jock who was taking three magnifying glasses of varying size and a jeweller's eyeglass from the pockets of his safari jacket and lining them up on the bar. 'You an expert?'

'I know something of gemstones,' said Jock.

'Yeah?' He paused, thinking with some difficulty. 'Won it in a card game. The only finger it'll fit on.' He took it off slowly and handed it to Jock. 'Often wondered what it was worth. The bloke swore it was a fair dinkum ruby.' Then he added warningly, 'I wouldn't try to nick it if I was you.'

Jock just gave him a look, then made what I thought was for him a considerable performance of examining the stone closely through each of the magnifying glasses in turn, and finally the jeweller's eyeglass, while making occasional grunting sounds. Then he passed the ring back to the stockman with exaggerated care.

'What ya reckon it's worth?' the big man said.

'I don't value stones,' said Jock. 'I'm not an assessor. I'll just say this. . .you should take good care of it, very—good—care. Best of luck.' Jock gave the stockman a friendly wave and we headed for the door leaving the big man staring at the ring as if seeing it for the first time.

As we drove east up the valley, I looked at Jock and said, 'Is it a very valuable stone?'

'Paste,' said Jock without changing his expression or taking his eyes off the road.

Jock dug a very fine hole. By Saturday night he was waist deep; by Sunday night his eyes could just see over the edge; by the time we left on Monday afternoon his raised hand touched the rim. It was the sort of hole a man could be proud of. It was surrounded by piles of dirt and a little pile of rocks he had chipped with his geologist's hammer.

Jock looked longingly back at the hole as we walked away each carrying a bag of rock samples. 'I'd say it has promise,' he said. 'I must check on when the next long weekend is.'

He said 'Thank you for coming,' as I left him to walk down the path to the cottage, but I sensed that as a mere chief cook and bottlewasher, tent erecter, hewer of wood and drawer of water I was something of a disappointment to him. He had after all put in a second set of picks, shovels, crowbars, etc. etc. etc.

10

It's no easy matter to out-sit a duck

I settled comfortably on the high stool behind the kitchen curtains; I knew I could be there for some time. It's no easy matter to out-sit a duck. Ducks are experts at sitting; they devote nine-tenths of their lives to sitting. But I was determined to solve the mystery. Over the previous couple of weeks Dora had been missing at intervals for days on end. I had been putting out food and water as usual and it had been eaten and drunk, but whether by Dora or by seagulls or possums or bush rats I did not know. On the few occasions I had seen Dora, she had simply appeared, as she had now, on the duck house patio, and after eating and drinking her fill had disappeared again without a sound. I had begun to feel churlish about this. If she were going to rely on me for sustenance, the least she could do was give a decorative fly-past every now and then.

I squinted through the narrow gap in the curtains. My backside was numb from perching on the stool. Dora finished her preening, flapped her wings to settle the individual feathers in place, then waddled down the ramp onto the rock, flopped into the water, and paddled across to a small patch of land, overgrown with prickly lantana scrub, which abutted the Dennises' house on my left. She scrambled up the rocky face, pushed her way through a tangle of dead branches and flotsam, and disappeared in the lantana.

So she's got a nest! And here you've been wondering why she hasn't been laying. Of course she wouldn't lay in the duck house where you can snatch her eggs from her. She's picked her own spot.

Then it really hit me. She's sitting on a clutch of eggs! What are you going to do with ducklings?

The tide was only half in. I whipped off my shoes and socks, rolled up my trousers, ran down on to the rock, and waded across to the patch of land. I got down on my hands and knees and, following Dora's tracks, pushed my way through the lantana.

The term 'clutch' is hopelessly inadequate. Dora was encircled by eggs like strings of outrageously large imitation pearls.

Weeks went by; obviously the eggs weren't fertile. But Dora wouldn't leave the nest; her food and water remained untouched. She was thin and scrawny, her red wattles and beak had lost nearly all their colour, her feathers were the texture of dead grass. When she stood she tottered pitifully.

I became as broody as Dora as I worked with the kitchen window open, one ear cocked for the sound of cheeps from the patch of land covered with lantana. I thought of her urgent flights around the harbour, her fruitless searching for a mate, and I mourned for her. She hadn't found her duck equivalent of a knight in shining armour. She sat on her eggs like an aging, unloved spinster with her collection of childhood dolls.

But perhaps more than anything I was appalled by the waste of time and effort. Grimly, I reached a conclusion: if you've got to have one duck, then why the hell not have two? If a human being can adopt a child, why shouldn't a duck adopt a duckling?

I changed down into second gear to drive across the low wooden bridge spanning the creek, then crawled along the unformed tree-lined dirt road, rolling into and out of deep potholes, weaving my way through scattered sharp-edged rocks.

The deep-voiced boy who had answered the phone had

said in the approved country fashion, 'Once you get on the road you can't miss it, mister.' For once, such a direction was accurate; the road didn't go anywhere other than to the farm.

It had taken seven or eight phone calls and the best part of a morning to locate someone with a supply of day-old ducklings. I could have had young ducks 'just right for the table' or 'about gettin' t' the leggy stage', or I could have 'hung on for a coupla weeks until a batch came out'. None of these alternatives suited Dora. She wanted a newly hatched duckling—now.

Eventually, I passed through a fence where a gate drooped open on its hinges; I crossed a paddock and drove carefully through the mixed flocks of geese, chickens and ducks surrounding an unpainted weatherboard house that drooped as sadly as the front gate. The heads of children appeared over the verandah railing, at windows and around doors. The biggest girl said, 'Are you the man who rang about the duckling?' A little boy, whose chin just topped the railing, tittered.

'Yes,' I said, ignoring the latter.

'It'll cost you twenty cents,' said the girl.

'That's all right,' I said, mentally noting that it was costing me dollars in lost working time. 'It's up here. We got it ready for you.'

The geese hissed at me as I walked through them to the verandah. A little yellow creature with a black cap on its head and Charlie Chaplin-sized yellow feet was hurling itself against the sides of a cardboard carton, featherless stubs of wings flapping as it fought to get out. I looked at it dubiously, then spoke to the biggest girl who was holding the carton. 'May I see your father?'

'He's out,' she said.

'Your mother then?'

'She's out, too.'

'I see.' I glanced at the assorted collection of poultry parading and scratching around the house, then examined the wildly cheeping captive in the carton. 'Are you sure it's a duck?'

'Sure, mister.'

'It has a black cap on its head.'

'Lots of them have. Honest.'

'They have? It's not a goose?'

I thought the little boy who had tittered would have hysterics. He screwed up his eyes, crossed his legs and doubled up with laughter.

'No, mister,' the biggest girl said and, pointing at the monsters among the assorted poultry, added, '*they're* geese.'

'I know that. I just don't want this,' pointing at the bouncing dob of yellow in the carton, 'to look like them when it grows up.'

'No, it can't, mister. See! There's its mother.' The girl pointed to a Dora-type Muscovy surrounded by ducklings which had emerged from under the house. I considered the mass of ducklings. Several had black caps on their heads; every one had enormous feet. 'Are they *all* hers?'

'Yes, mister.'

'There's an awful lot.'

'Sure. They have millions.'

I looked closely at my twenty-cent purchase and compared it with the brood around the white Muscovy. 'Yes, I can see it's a duckling.' Then I peered at it even more closely, not really knowing what physiological feature I was looking for. 'I said on the phone that I wanted a duck, that is, a female. You're sure this is a female duck and not a drake?'

'Jeez, mister,' said one of the boys, 'how would *we* know?'

The biggest girl walloped him smartly across an ear. 'How would *you* know? *You* don't know *anything*.' And addressing me with total self-assurance, she said, 'It's a duck all right, mister.'

'You're sure?'

'Of course I'm sure.' She shook the arm of a smaller sister. 'Tell him how I knew about the kittens.'

'She knew about the kittens, mister.'

'She did?' I said. I looked into the carton again. 'About this black cap. . .' (I realised I was labouring the question, but I knew what I wanted for Dora—a daughter who would grow into a pleasant lady companion.) 'A Muscovy duck I know, a *female* duck, is pure white. . .'

'But lots of Muscovies have bits of black, mister. *Any* Muscovy can have black anywhere.' I vaguely recalled that *Duck Raising* said something to this effect.

The boy who had been walloped was still rubbing his ear. 'Why don't you want a drake, mister? They're bigger.'

He jumped back as his sister threw another haymaker. 'Because a drake doesn't lay eggs, stupid, that's why.'

The smallest boy had his eyes screwed up again, his legs were crossed, and he was doubled up with laughter.

'If you're not careful,' I began, 'you'll. . .'

'He's always doing it,' the biggest girl interrupted.

'I'm not surprised,' I said. The duckling in the carton was still taking blind running jumps at the vertical sides, crashing heavily to the bottom after each attempt to escape. I looked at it anxiously. 'How can I stop it from leaping around? It's going to batter itself to pulp.'

'No it won't, mister,' said another boy with an extraordinarily deep voice; I guessed it was he who had answered the phone. 'They're *tough*!'

'But it might break a leg or something.'

'Nah! You'd have to hit it with an axe.'

I winced. By now the important question on sex had been well sidetracked. I decided to accept the eldest girl's word for it; she seemed to know what she was talking about. The littlest girl began pummelling my leg purposefully to attract attention. 'Why do you only want *one* duckling, mister? Nobody else ever buys only *one* duckling.'

I drew a deep breath. 'Well, I have. . .' Out of the corner of an eye I could see her brother, eyes bright with expectancy, already wrapping one leg around the other, and I wilted. 'I have a little girl just like you and I'm buying the duckling for her.' There's a time and a place for raw truth. I felt sure that Dora would understand.

Squire Wilcox's wife Joyce was hanging out washing as I walked down the path to my cottage. I called to her: 'Congratulate me. I'm a father.' Even with a mouth full of clothes pegs her face became wonderfully womanly and seemed to radiate light like a painted Byzantine saint. 'Oh, how. . .' she began after spitting out the clothes pegs, then the light suddenly went out as she recalled my lack of marital status.

'Do you want to see it?' I said.

She fiddled with the clothes pegs, swallowed and looked nervously at the cardboard carton under my arm. 'Errr. . .'

'Here, I'll show you. It's a girl. She's got feet like Charlie Chaplin, so I've called her Charlotte.'

Joyce is a pleasant woman; it was one of the few times I'd seen her without a smile. I opened up the carton. Immediately, the duckling made another attack on the cardboard precipice. 'Oh, isn't it sweet.' The light around her head was switched on again. 'Don. . . Dad!' she called. 'Do come and see this.'

I could hear Don under the house. He was all but wedged under the section right at the back—or was it the front—which was close to ground level. He was painstakingly jacking up centimetre by centimetre the entire rear area, now the kitchen and bathroom, that had once been an added-on verandah-cum-kitchen like the Muirs'. It had sagged over the years, a fact that was irritatingly rammed home to Don every time he stood at the kitchen sink doing the washing up. The window above the sink that he was forced to look at had a pronounced list to port. This, he could not tolerate. The Squire was a perfectionist.

No doubt glad of a chance for a breather, Don crawled out looking like a miner coming off shift, followed by his father, Walter, now eighty, who was working with him.

Both peered into the carton at Charlotte huddled in a corner. She also was having a breather.

'Ah, the entree,' said Don.

'Wouldn't make a main course,' said Walter, he who chanted, 'Peas, parsnips, potatoes' at Dora.

'You realise I'll have to up the rent,' Don said. 'Our contract is for a residence; a poultry farm will cost extra.'

'She's to be a companion for Dora. You know she's been sitting on eggs for what seems like months.'

Walter grunted. 'You're wasting your time,' he said.

This was all too true, but I echoed it just the same.
'Wasting my time?'
'Yes, wasting your time. Dora won't have it; she'll kill it.'
'Surely not.'
'If she doesn't, I'll be surprised. I've kept ducks you know.'

I did know. I also knew that to date the good man had been unable to answer with certainty any of the many questions I had put to him about duck-keeping and had drawn the conclusion that his duck-keeping had been pretty haphazard. But Walter was answering with certainty now. 'You've got just one chance,' he said. 'Timing's the thing. Dora's got to think it's hers. Wait until it's nearly dark, then push her off her eggs, grab them, and immediately pop the duckling in the nest. She'll be confused, but she'll settle down for the night, and by the time morning's come she'll have convinced herself the duckling's hers.'

It made sense. I had heard stories about birds rejecting their own offspring, so it was reasonable to assume that a domestic duck would be chary about adopting a foundling, particularly after weeks and weeks of frustrated sitting. I decided to take Walter's advice.

It was high tide when I waded across in the dark, holding the carton and a plastic bucket up high as I shone the torch into the water and calculated the speed at which I could leap onto the oyster-covered rocks should I see anything vaguely resembling the shape of a shark.

I clambered onto the patch of land and, pushing the carton and plastic bucket ahead of me, crawled through the tunnel in the lantana. I went straight to work. I pushed Dora back off the nest, and she staggered on her wobbly legs, feeble from weeks of sitting. She cheeped distressingly and pecked weakly at my hand as I picked up her eggs one by one and put them in the plastic bucket. Then I opened the lid of the carton, grabbed the duckling and put it in the nest ready to snatch it up should she attempt to attack it.

Dora cocked her head and looked at the duckling. Her eye popped, her beak fell open and her amazed expression clearly said, 'So *that's* how it's done!'

Young Charlotte cheeped and ran to her.

Dora spread her wings to cover the duckling; then, with new vigour, she lashed at me with her beak, crest erect, hissing threats.

Hurriedly, I crawled out through the tunnel. As I waded back through the water, I could hear mother and daughter cheeping to one another, and I felt a new understanding of the compulsion of young fathers to rush out and buy bottles of champagne.

11

'Gotta bit o' the dingo in 'im?'

'Listen, Old Untameable, I want to know how you do it. Don't just stand there laughing at me knowing you're a dingo Houdini. How *do* you get out of it?'

Rummy continued to laugh pleasantly at me—a reasonable interpretation of his lolling tongue and bright eyes—his muzzle once more dangling like a Highlander's sporran from the clip on his collar. He reached out a white paw and tapped my leg as though he was aware that I was a mere valet charged with dressing and undressing. The demarcation line between dog and deputy master was extremely grey. At times it was very clear that Rummy was the boss.

I squatted, unclipped the muzzle and, no doubt to his chagrin, put it back on, refastened the strap around his neck and again clipped the muzzle to the collar. I then tugged it this way and that, the way I had seen him worry at it with a paw but I just couldn't see how he could extend the strap the length of his snout to get the muzzle off.

But he did. Over the week I had been minding him since Jack and Jean had left on a field trip with a group of gem-mologists, every second or third time he went for a walk he returned with the muzzle dangling from the clip.

That afternoon I was staring at the curtains mulling over just how I would tackle a story when he got up from his blanket beside my desk, walked silently to the door and put his nose to the crack. This had become part of a pattern. He stood there for some time while I continued to stare at the curtains. Then, aware that I was deliberately ignoring him, he returned to his blanket, picked up the muzzle which lay beside it and pushed it against my leg, just as a glimmer of light was shining through on the story treatment.

It's hard to ignore a dingo pushing a wire cage against your leg. The glimmer began to fade, shook about a bit, then disappeared like the image on a switched-off television screen. I sighed at the loss and turned to my alternative task of dingo minding.

As Rummy wandered off up the path to commence his social round I felt a tinge of envy of his free-and-easy lifestyle. Hey, I said to myself, you want to know how Rummy gets his muzzle off: why don't you follow him? You can think just as effectively 'tailing' a dingo as staring at the curtains.

So, with a clear conscience and a sense of purpose I thrust a notebook in a pocket and proceeded to climb the hill.

Rummy was a little way along the street, leg cocked, marking a clump of grass. I stood and watched as in quick succession he then claimed as his own an hibiscus shrub, a letterbox on a stick and a streetlight pole until now believed to be the property of the Electricity Commission.

But was that what it all meant? I took out my notebook and scribbled, *Check leg cocking*, a crisp notation that might puzzle me somewhat when I came across it again in six months' time. Perhaps I was wrong in believing that the compulsion to pee on every object a dog passes is marking territory. They say it does in the wild, but did it here in suburbia where there's such a mixed bag of well-fed, pampered mutts? Perhaps it is more akin to graffiti scrawled with a felt pen on a public lavatory wall saying, *Barney Bloggs was here*. No more, no less. The simple statement of a simple man that here, on the porcelain tiles he, Barney Bloggs, had made his mark.

It must be extremely confusing in suburbia with 25 dogs all laying claim to every object jutting above ground. Then I got to thinking about how it works in the wild.

Case history: strange dingo, wolf or whatever wandering through the scrub suddenly props at scent on a tree trunk. It's a mighty powerful scent; could mean heap big trouble for a dingo, wolf or whatever stepping over the line.

But where is the line? Does the territory claimed extend back from the side on which the tree is marked or in the other direction on the opposite side. There was a 180-degree margin for error here.

I added to *Check leg cocking. . .Check geographic boundaries*.

Roy Kennedy, the gardening Mole from the high side of the crescent whom I had met in the butcher's shop, was walking across the road carrying a shovel parallel with the ground with some care. Our paths intersected at the lawned area fronting Bruce Pearce's house which adjoined the Muirs' land. 'Afternoon,' Roy said crisply, and passing in front of me, held out the shovel above the lawn and turned it over. 'That's back where it belongs,' he said.

I looked down at the lawn and raised an inquiring eyebrow.

'Blackie,' said Roy. 'He comes over to *my* garden. Does it every day.'

'So you return to Bruce that which you consider is rightfully his. Does he know you do this?'

'Yes, I've told him.'

'Doesn't he get mad?'

'No. He knows it's his dog's poo. I told him that by rights he should come and pick it up. He just smiled. That's Bruce.'

I thought of Rummy presently reasserting his claim to two-thirds of the street. 'Does Rummy do the same thing? I'm looking after him while Jock's away.'

'The dingo? No. He hasn't come in since I turned the hose on him years ago. But then I don't think he ever did.'

This was one of the few occasions on which I heard Rummy spoken of as a dingo. I found it interesting that so few picked his breed. I guess city people just don't expect to see a dingo with a price on its head wandering amiably around suburbia.

I mused that even in the country, despite Jock's concerns, Rummy was usually accepted as just another dog, although there would be comments, 'Gotta bit o' the dingo in 'im, hasn't he?' In the wild, most dingoes have a tuckered-up look due no doubt to uncertain hunting. Rummy's well-fleshed body set him apart from his breed.

On one of the rare occasions Jock did take Rummy bush, he was camping in the ranges on the South Coast of New South Wales. One of the locals joined the party around the campfire in the evening and talk got around to dingoes and the blight they were to stock owners in the district. Jock, in the way he would, deliberately drew the man who laid claim to being something of an authority on dingoes, about their nasty habits and their untameability. Throughout the conversation Rummy lay contentedly beside Jock, head on paws, nose to the fire.

The fact is a great number of the ragtag dogs that are used so effectively to work sheep and cattle have 'got a bit of the dingo in them'. Although most dogs on sheep and cattle stations are chained up at night—indeed for much of the time when they are not being used to work stock—it is not uncommon for an unchained dog to go out on the town after nightfall, particularly when there is a full moon. If there are dingoes in an adjoining forest, inevitably they meet up: should a station bitch happen to be on heat a litter of dingo-cross pups is likely. It is even speculated that only a quarter of the wild dogs in the eastern regions of Australia and three-quarters of the number inland, are pure dingoes.

Many sheep and cattlemen contend that stock losses attributed to pure dingoes frequently are the work of crossbreeds and station dogs gone wild. Nonetheless, one of Australia's most effective work dogs, the blue speckle cattle dog or blue heeler, was developed from dingo strain.

By now, Rummy had disappeared up the driveway of a house and it suddenly occurred to me that there could be human intervention in the removal of the muzzle. Since being appointed deputy master I had learned that Rummy had a large circle of friends over a wide area and enjoyed dropping in for a chat and a pat. I didn't like to see him muzzled, so obviously others didn't either. Elementary, my dear Watson. Who lived there? I didn't have the faintest idea: after all, the house was on the high side of the road, the *other* side. Well, whoever it was, as deputy master I would have to have a word with them if need be about the necessity for Rummy to wear his muzzle.

A couple of minutes ticked by and it became apparent that I wasn't cut out to be a private detective tailing suspects. You see them in the movies standing under lamp posts for hours, shadowy figures invariably with a plume of cigarette smoke streaming up to the top edge of the screen. Whatever do they think about standing there, standing there, standing there. . .?

Then I reminded myself that *I* had plenty to think about, whipped myself back to the story I was working on and actually was jotting down some sketchy notes as I leaned against a tree when Rummy trotted back down the drive-way—still wearing his muzzle. So much for human intervention in that house. He had made a purely social call.

Rummy proceeded down the street at a steady trot with the air of a dog confidently going about his business. Further along, a couple of boys released from school were playing ball on the roadway. One of them whistled and called, 'Hey, Rummy! Here, boy!' and when Rummy trotted up to him he got down on his knees and made faces at Rummy caged in his muzzle and tugged his ears. This obviously was a game they had played before. Were the boys the culprits? Did they take off his muzzle so he could join in their ball game?

But I knew that he wasn't all that keen on the games that humans traditionally cook up for their dogs to play. Chasing the ball, you-chase-me-I-chase-you, retrieving the stick and the like didn't amuse Rummy. He wasn't a tricks dog. Throw a stick and his response to your urgings was a look which seemed to imply, 'You threw it; you go get it'.

His one performance—taking a biscuit extended from Jock's lips or waiting for the okay to get at one balanced on his own nose—had a practical aspect. He tolerated the non-sense for the sake of the biscuit.

At a command he would sit up on his haunches to please Jock, but he never looked comfortable. It was as though he was thinking, it just ain't natural to sit this way. I feel sure that had he been aware that the human term for the trick is 'begging' he would have politely but firmly declined to perform.

A couple of ear scratches from the boys and Rummy was off again.

Just before the corner of the street a dog started barking frantically from behind a fence. Ah ah! I hope the gate's shut. This was Rummy's bête noire and the principal reason he had to wear his muzzle—a red kelpie with whom he had battled again and again to assert his authority as top dog of the district. The gate was shut, but the kelpie hurled itself against the slats as Rummy calmly cocked a leg on a clump of grass then stood and looked at his archenemy as if to say, 'Come out from behind that fence and even with my muzzle on I'll lick you with one paw tied behind my back'.

I don't know how the notion that a dingo is cowardly got started, let alone accepted into the idiom of Australian language. To call someone 'a dingo' is scraping the bottom of the epithet barrel. Perhaps the unfounded reputation stems from the dingo's elusiveness in the bush, its reluctance to confront people. To me, this is simply proof of the dogs's intelligence: it knows that in a serious confrontation it won't win.

Giving the lie to the reputation for cowardice are many stories of the courage of the dingo. Trappers say that a dog caught in a trap won't howl or cringe: it will calmly look a man in the eye as he raises his rifle, pulls the trigger.

Trapped dogs, such as Peg Leg in the Aramac district of Central Queensland, have been known to gnaw off their own legs in order to escape. A bitch, Peg Leg was hunted for three years before she was shot. They took 36 shotgun pellets from her shoulders.

Bumblefoot was another three-legged dingo that was hounded for eight years in the Chinchilla Shire in Queensland. He was finally worn down after an all-out hunt lasting nearly three weeks.

Although Rummy was a fierce fighter he wasn't a bully. He seemed to fight only when challenged to establish dominance. He was, in fact, remarkably tolerant. He accepted the strange dogs that were brought into the house by his master's friends; he was forebearing of small dogs and puppies. Repeatedly, he was verbally attacked by the Dennises' Australian terrier, Archie. Rummy would stand and look down with a puzzled expression as the diminuitive Archie rushed around—and sometimes under—him, yapping furiously, baring his teeth, nipping the air.

Just now, Rummy had no time to waste on the kelpie that was expressing its outrage at the territorial claims being made to the footpath outside *its* fence. He simply scratched the ground vigorously a few times then, with tail raised, trotted off jauntily around the corner. By the time I reached the second corner Rummy was bounding toward another dog halfway along the street. So, he had an assignation with Twink!

Twink was a charming young boxer bitch who was a frequent caller at the cottage. I had no illusions that she came to see me: she clearly just dropped by in the hope of seeing Rummy. Soon, the two were lolloping around the way dogs do and knowing that this could go on for half an hour I took a turn up a side street, smartened my thus-far leisurely pace and strode off, purposefully converting my investigatory walk into a worthwhile constitutional walk.

Ten minutes later, after circumnavigating a couple of blocks I was back in the same street. The two dogs were still lolloping around each other, Twink mouthing Rummy's neck with her great jaws.

Then Rummy drew back and began pushing at the muzzle with a paw. It was apparent that it was irritating him because he couldn't mouth Twink.

After abortively swiping at the muzzle with his paw a number of times Rummy walked up to Twink, stood squarely in front of her and deliberately pushed the wire cage against the boxer's flat face. She backed away, but Rummy followed, pushing persistently. This must have been most uncomfortable for Twink.

Finally, she opened her big jaws and fastened on the end of the muzzle. That obviously was what Rummy wanted. He

immediately pulled back, and so did Twink. Together, they heaved as if in a tug-of-war, at the same time vigorously shaking their heads.

Soon, the strap holding the muzzle was dragged over Rummy's ears and he was free of it. The two of them resumed their romp unconcerned by the swinging 'sporran' clipped to Rummy's collar.

Question answered.

12

A great front yard

The barbecue fire glowed at the end of the terrace; a possum could be heard moving through the trees; from along the bay came the soft 'oomp, oomp, oomp' of a tawny frogmouth, an owl-like night bird, proclaiming, I assume, his love for his mate; above us, silhouetted against a full silver moon, the figures of fruit bats flying from across the harbour to eat the fruit of a giant Moreton Bay fig tree growing on the edge of the bank near the head of the bay; below us, not far out from the jetty, the little ketch I had bought not long before riding at her mooring.

It gives a special pleasure to look out at your own boat, equipped and ready to sail at a few minutes notice. She was a sweet craft, a Hereschoff-designed H28, a planked 28-foot ketch with timber masts, an ample, comfortable cockpit and a varnished cabin that glowed. A cruising boat—not built for racing close-hauled in a field of fanatics who would all but kill to get there first—she was well rigged, steady and dry in a sea. Like a ten year old, I was going to keep her for ever and ever.

I had spent an idyllic day sailing in Middle Harbour with Jock and Jean Muir and a couple of other friends, running before a steady sou'easter past the houses that cling to the steep hillside and the charming cottages and converted boat-sheds down by the water inhabited by Ratties, along past the wooded shoreline that leads to Bantry Bay and the thick-walled sheds set into the hillside where gelignite was stored after the hulks had been abandoned. And on up the long reach of Roseville Chase that shallows not far beyond the old Killarney picnic ground where, half a century before, ferries brought weekend merrymakers to drink beer and tea on the grassy slopes and dance polkas, waltzes and military twosteps in the weatherboard hall, its galvanised iron roof sadly sagging these days. Then going right about to work back down the Chase into the wind, novice crew alert for my cries of 'Ready about!. . .Lee oh!' as tack succeeded tack. And dropping anchor to lunch off a sandy beach laid bare by the falling tide in a tiny bay fed by a freshwater stream.

All this was my 'front yard'.

Now, in the evening, we were sitting on the terrace alongside the cottage sipping white wine after a feast of mussels which had been picked from the jetty piles and cooked over the open fire, and fish barbecued in aluminium foil. Soon, someone began humming a tune, then others took up the chorus.

When I got up to put more wood on the fire and poke it around a bit the leaves in the tree above me rustled. I looked up, expecting to see an extrovert brushtail with hopes of a handout. Instead, I saw a little round face with small, neat ears and a pair of soft eyes shining in the firelight. It was a ringtail, or *Pseudocheirus peregrinus*, as the Sydney species is formally known. While not a rare species there are far fewer ringtail possums than brushtails in the Sydney area, and as they are shy they are seen less frequently. Over its shoulder could be seen the even smaller face of a baby clinging to its back. We made appreciative noises and it obligingly moved forward so that we could see its tiny offspring more clearly, the mother curling her slim, white-tipped, whip-like tail around the branch for support. But it would come no closer, refusing to be lured by offerings of lettuce. I knew it preferred the leaves and blossoms of the native lilly-pilly tree a little way up the hillside.

Perhaps half an hour later I got that 'I'm-being-watched'

feeling and to my surprise saw a pair of eyes reflecting in the light of the fire on the stone steps on the level above the terrace. 'Hello ringtail,' I said coaxingly. 'You are brave coming down to the ground. So you do want some lettuce.' But the eyes disappeared.

'Down, boy!' Jock said softly. Rummy had risen to his feet at the sound of my talking-to-animals voice and was staring at the spot where the eyes had been. They reappeared and his tail moved a little in a wagging motion. This was strange because he was wary of possums after the encounter that had injured his eye. The pair of eyes disappeared again into the dark but when I made a come-hither sound through pursed lips they could again be seen peering around a stone block.

'Oh, it's a cat,' said Jean.

'Is it Nicky? Rummy seems to know it.'

'He knows every dog and cat in the district. No, it's not Nicky. It might be a wild cat—but Rummy's probably met it.'

Which was true enough. Rummy actually liked cats. Nicky, the Muirs' ginger tom, was his close friend. They played games, groomed each other, curled up to sleep together. Every day, he made a point of rubbing noses by way of saying good morning to the big black cat that lived next door on the other side with his labrador pal, Blackie. Perhaps because dingoes don't have an historical association with cats he had never learned that they're supposed to be dogs' enemies. Repeatedly, he would trot amiably up to some strange moggie, wagging his tail, only to encounter raking claws. He never retaliated; after a yelp of pain he would look at the cat with great puzzlement.

A small grey shape had formed behind the eyes, half crouching, ready to flee. I tossed up a scrap of fish left over from the barbecue. The cat moved forward quickly, snatched it up, merged with the night. It returned several times for more fish but could be coaxed no closer.

The following evening I stepped out of the door heading for the detached room with the stained-glass window, when I again saw the cat on the steps ahead of me. I stopped and looked up at it. It regarded me warily but didn't attempt to run away.

'Umm, you're only a little cat,' I said by way of making conversation. 'And you're a very pretty little cat.' It had striped tabby markings but its fur was silver-grey. Its face was small and pleasant despite the wary look. But I thought I should clarify the situation. 'You've been misinformed,' I said. 'There's no barbecue tonight.' Then I remembered that a bottle of milk was almost empty and so was unnecessarily taking up space in the refrigerator. On impulse, I went back inside, poured the remaining milk into a saucer, brought it out, put it down a little way along the path, then moved back to the doorway.

The cat approached the bowl cautiously and began lapping the milk looking up at me at intervals. 'So, you're hungry,' I said. 'Do you live around here? Do you belong to a family or are you a wild cat?' Somehow the one-sided conversation sounded vaguely familar to me as though I had had it with someone before.

Then I thought of the loin lamb chops on the kitchen bench alongside the potatoes I had just peeled to cook for my dinner. It's a weakness, I know, but I always succumb to eating the 'tails' of loin lamb chops, the bits that curl at the end of the chop proper and which butchers no doubt regard highly because they make up the weight. I know the tails can't be good for me, that they contain too much fat, that health-conscious friends pointedly cut them off and push them to the side of their plates, and that I sneak covetous glances at them the way I do crisp bacon rinds treated similarly by the self-righteous. Well, here was an opportunity for an exercise in self-discipline that unquestionably would be to my benefit.

I went back into the kitchen, cut off the loin chop tails, put them on another saucer and left it outside the door. The saucers were empty, licked clean, when I collected them later while doing the washing up.

By now, it should be apparent that I had absolutely no intention of keeping pets. I was prepared to act as deputy master to a dingo and occasional provider to a couple of ducks, but there I propped.

The next morning I looked up from my desk to see the little cat lying on the terrace. It was on its back, paws in the air, the sun shining on belly fur that was glistening silver rather than grey. This was the first time I had seen the cat in daylight. With its contrasting black tabby stripes it was, as I had observed earlier, an unusually pretty animal.

The cat developed something of a habit of lying on the terrace, which I accepted. After all, the Muirs' ginger cat Nicky would sit on the awning above the doorway peering at me through the skylight while I worked; Rummy would drop in several times a day and flop down by my desk; Blackie, the labrador from two doors along, would call by; Archie, the Dennises' Australian terrier would amble over for an occasional ear scratch; and Dora and Charlotte paddled up and down the foreshore and swam around below me. So far as I was concerned, the situation was quite satisfactory: all care but no responsibility.

As time passed, I noticed with some satisfaction that the little cat was far less scrawny. In fact, it was getting nicely rounded, which I attributed to what by now had become one good meal a day. Then it became apparent that the improved physical condition was not attributable purely to food.

Weeks went by and I found myself calling Little Cat, Big Cat. Then one night there she was on the doorstep wearing her old slim figure.

I searched everywhere: in groves of trees and clumps of bushes, under the houses of immediate neighbours, in garden sheds and discarded cardboard cartons. . . Of kittens there was nary a sign.

Clearly, Little Cat was holed up further afield, perhaps in the rainforest reserve at the end of the bay where she herself may have been dumped as a kitten.

I had crossed two neighbouring properties and was peering into the scrub on the side of the track that led from the end house up through the bush to the roadway when I realised I was being watched by a boy who had been walking down the track.

'Have you lost something?' he asked.

'Not lost,' I said. 'I've never found them.' And I explained what I was about.

The boy wrinkled up his face in thought. 'It sounds like Blossom Richardson,' he said.

'Who? What?' I said.

'Blossom Richardson. I know she's had kittens.' He pointed through the bush to the tip of the roof of a house I had never realised was there. 'The path leads off this track further up the hill.'

Six cats of varying size and colour were tearing at a fish that had been tossed on to a patch of grass at the rear of the house. A seventh cat, a pretty little silver-grey tabby was sitting watching from the sideline: there was no room for her at the inn. The heads of four kittens peered from beneath a nearby shed.

A woman came to the door. I explained why I was there. Blossom Richardson looked up at me unblinking. 'I've never seen you in my life before,' she clearly said.

13

The grandfather of octuplets

The girl on the farm may have been an authority on kitten sexing, but she had a lot to learn about ducks.

Charlotte grew into an enormous drake twice the size of Dora, with handsome red wattles suggestive of the mutton-chop whiskers of a nineteenth-century cavalry officer and a bulb above his beak that had overtones of a whisky nose.

So Charlotte became Charlie. He was *all* male, which means, according to your views on this subject, that he could be described as a strong leader, a worthy trencherman and a lusty lover—or as a flat-footed, overbearing boofhead with two insatiable appetites, one of them gastronomic.

At first it bothered me. It seemed like, well, incest. But I rationalised that there was not any bloodline, after all Charlie was adopted. I didn't know how that put things in law, human law that is, but it certainly put a different complexion on things in general. Had they simply met in a casual way and become friends then it would not have mattered at all.

Whichever way I cared to look at it, the indisputable fact was that Dora and Charlie had become romantically involved. Not that I could see much romance in it for Dora. The mating game for ducks is very direct and there is no doubt left that in the duck world the female is the weaker of the sexes.

But undoubtedly Charlie had charm; women and children in particular found him quite irresistible. I handled him as little as possible, not only because I am allergic to feathers, but because I felt that his chances of survival were greater if he had a deep distrust of human beings.

For some reason I had failed to get this point across to him. The difficulty with Charlie was not in catching him, but in booting him out of the way to get past him as he sat contentedly at the foot of the steps. Children would rush up to him and pat him and feed him wheat from their grubby little hands, and he would alternately wag his tail and raise his black-capped crest so that he looked very fierce, whereupon the children would cry out with delight, 'Isn't he beautiful'—which must have been shattering to Charlie's male ego, especially after being brought up as a girl.

While this was going on, Dora would perch on the far end of the rock, her nervously flicking wings suggesting the beat of an idling engine of a plane ready for a smart take-off. She knew all about human beings.

Charlie had learned to fly, but he never achieved even Dora's standard of proficiency. His build was against it, dictating that all his missions be in the low-level, short-range class. This was something of a disappointment to me, as I had been rather looking forward to watching the pair of them doing some spectacular formation flying around the bay. As it was, his trickiest performance was landing on one of the plate-sized jetty posts on which he perched for the night while Dora perched on the other.

I waited until the three hard-boiled hen eggs were cold, put them in different pockets, peeped quickly through the curtains to check that Dora and Charlie were still foraging among the seagulls on the sandflat, then went downstairs and crossed to the patch of land where Dora had made her nest. The land was now virtually clear of lantana scrub; two pairs of big feet and a pair of foraging bills had done as thorough a job as a machete and mattock. There were three eggs in Dora's nest: one had been laid that morning, the others on the preceding two days. I picked up the eggs and replaced them with the three hard-boiled hen eggs.

It was all so easy. What Walter Wilcox—he who had bred ducks—had told me was proving true: a duck gets confused when it has to deal with any number greater than three. (I can understand this; I'm much the same.) So long as I left three eggs in her nest, the old gentleman had said, Dora would keep on laying determinedly to make up the number necessary for a clutch. Just how she calculated the number, I don't know. Perhaps she measured herself against the circumference of the clutch; the fact that she hadn't known when to stop on her first effort could be attributed to inexperience.

The system worked splendidly for a week or more, then for several days in a row there was no fourth egg in the nest. Had she stopped laying, or was she aware of what was going on?

I scouted around and found another nest among the tangle of debris. So, I thought, I've underestimated your intelligence. You *can* tell the difference between a hen egg and a duck egg.

I hard-boiled three duck eggs, marked each end with a pencilled cross and placed them in her new nest. Again, the system worked for a week or more before Dora proved not only that she knew the difference between a hen egg and a duck egg but that she could count past three.

The game of treasure hunt continued, both bird and man growing wilier as the weeks went by.

Then the game ended. Dora refused to play; she had run out of space on the little patch of land.

'Dora,' I said, 'you're looking a wreck. You're positively grubby and your feathers need preening. Come to think of it, I haven't seen you swimming for days. You'll have to smarten up.' She merely gave me one of her nasty looks, calculated, I felt sure, to give my conscience a jab; she knew who had been stealing her eggs.

I went back to my desk and started typing. Nothing much appeared on the paper. I rested my chin on my fists and tried

squinting at the curtain pattern, but there wasn't much point
to pattern-gazing nowadays: all I could ever make out of the
pattern was Muscovy ducks in flight. Quickly I began typing,
'Peter picked a peck of pickled peppers while round the
rugged rocks the ragged rascal ran', but having run around
the rugged rocks, I could proceed no further.

A cup of coffee, I thought, breaking a golden rule. That'll
do the trick: a cup of good strong coffee. Purposefully, I strode
across to the kitchen, turned on the tap full blast to fill the
electric jug, and snapped on the switch. The psychology of
this is to create the impression that I'm really too busy creating
to find time for making cups of coffee.

I was drumming my fingers on the windowpane gazing at
nothing while impatiently waiting for the jug to boil when
suddenly I saw Dora's head stuck on the side of the cliff above
the duck house. It was like the stuffed head of an antelope
hanging on a wall. I blinked, and just as suddenly her head
disappeared, as though (to confuse the imagery) she had
whipped it back in through a ship's porthole. I blinked again,
then stared at the spot on the cliff; it was indistinguishable
from any other spot, being smothered in honeysuckle creeper.

I switched off the jug, crept down the stairs, and hidden
by the foundations of the house, scanned the cliff. Within a
minute or two Dora's head popped out through the creeper.
'Dora!' I shouted. 'What the blazes are you doing up there?'
She gave me one wild look and again disappeared. It was all
too clear what she was doing up there, and this was the reason
for her scruffy appearance. 'Listen,' I said, addressing the
honeysuckle, 'if *you* have time to scramble up and down cliffs,
I haven't. Do you expect me to put on climbing crampons to
collect your lousy eggs?' Quite obviously this was what she
was hoping to avoid. 'Anyway, if you do hatch a crop of
ducklings, how are you going to get them down? They're not
bloody seagulls.'

From the rock I examined the spot where her head had
disappeared. It was about a metre above the level of the roof
of the duck house; total height above water, more than two
metres. The cliff was nearly vertical.

I clambered onto the baulk of timber to which the duck house was nailed and parted the honeysuckle creeper. She was inside—at least, I assumed she was inside since I couldn't see her—what can only be described as a cave. The circumference of the entrance was little bigger than her girth. 'Dora!' I called. She didn't reply. Tentatively, I put a hand inside. It might have been a coal mine; I couldn't reach her. Then I heard a hiss and quickly withdrew my hand; it occurred to me that she could be sharing the cave with spiders, bats, blue-tongued lizards and venomous snakes.

They were all on the rock when I arrived home at midmorning: Charlie, Dora and a clump of bright yellow ducklings. A stiff wind was blowing from the southwest; misted spray flew from the wavelets which slapped at the oyster shells. The tide was rising.

'*Pat!*' I called to a colleague with whom I was collaborating on a script. I had just picked her up from across town and we had planned a busy day. She came running; I must have sounded as though I'd jammed a thumb in a door. 'What's wrong?'

'What's wrong? I'm the grandfather of octuplets.'

'They've *hatched*!' She pressed her nose against the window pane. 'Aren't they sweet.' From her, I'd have expected something more original. By now, I recognised 'Aren't they sweet' as the standard comment on ducklings. 'But how did she get them down there?' I had, of course, told her about the current situation.

'Only Dora, Charlie, the ducklings, a couple of seagulls and the good Lord, if he keeps an eye on this sort of thing, will ever know.'

I went downstairs to inspect the nest in case there were more ducklings still inside. As I sidled past her, Dora moved warily towards the edge of the rock, her proven escape route. The ducklings flowed after her, tiny balls of yellow down. I suppose she had good reason to regard me as a potential child murderer; after all, I had kept swiping her eggs. I climbed onto the timber to which the duck house was nailed and scrambled up the cliff. To my relief there were no more ducklings in the nest. As I slunk past her to return to the house, Dora moved even closer to the edge of the rock. The ducklings followed. I didn't dare look at her for fear she might take fright and fly off. The ducklings were teetering in the wind gusts on the lip of one of the several holes worn by the waves along the rock's outer edge and were being splashed by the spray.

Here on the foreshore, facing northwest, we took the full brunt of the westerly winds that blow right across the continent from the Indian Ocean to the Pacific in late winter. I always associate the month of August with the westerlies, although they can blow at strength from July through to September. Quite often the skies are clear, but on this August day the chill wind, which can be reminiscent of France's mistral, was blowing under layers of grey cloud.

We had papers well scattered around the room when I heard Lorna Dennis calling as she ran across the terrace, 'They've fallen in! The ducklings have fallen in!'

From the window we saw two splashes of yellow bobbing about in the water. The ducklings were paddling vigorously against the wind and the choppy waves, but still they were drifting backwards toward the jetty. Dora was perched on the edge of the rock, neck outstretched, clucking her agitated ducklings-come-home call, the rest of the brood huddled around her feet. 'Get back, Dora!' I shouted at her. 'Get back from the edge or you'll have the lot in.' She gave me one of her wild looks, then started revving her wings. '*Don't!*' I shouted. 'Don't fly off. Just stay there.'

'The butterfly net!' said Pat.

'The what?'

'Your butterfly net.'

'I don't own a butterfly net.'

'You do. The one you use to catch the fish.'

'The *landing* net? You're right.'

I ran to the spare room at the back of the cottage where I kept my fishing gear, grabbed the net, and ran down the steps. Paddling desperately, the ducklings were sailing backwards under the jetty. I made a play for one with the landing net, but it was just out of reach. Then Dora gave a loud cry and took off. She rushed straight past my head and landed with a plop between the two ducklings, squawking at me, 'Unhand my children!'

'Another one's in,' Lorna Dennis cried.

'Quick!' said Pat. 'Use the butterfly net.'

I was on my hands and knees on the jetty. I turned to see another yellow blob being tossed about near the oyster-covered rocks. The remaining five were swaying on the edge preparing to do lemming-like leaps in response to Dora's clucking behind me. 'Shut up!' I shouted at Dora. One duckling jumped into space, its unfeathered little wings flapping instinctively till it hit the water. The wind plays strange tricks in the bay rimmed as it is by cliffs; a gust raced toward us, and the two ducklings which had just gone in were tossed different ways and the four still on the rock were blown back from the edge.

Pat was now on the rock. 'Get between the ducklings and the water,' I called to her. Forgetting about the shark-warning notices, I jumped in, plunged chest-deep toward the duckling farthest from the shore, and scooped it up in the net. Then I scooped up the other.

Lorna came running down the steps with a cardboard carton. 'Good,' I called. 'We'll catch the lot while we're at it.'

I clambered ashore gingerly over the sharp oysters and emptied the two ducklings out of the net into the carton.

Dora had swum up behind me, bobbing about in the choppy sea, clucking furiously and glaring up at me as if I were to blame for everything. Fortunately, the two ducklings were on her lee side, sheltered somewhat from the wind, but they had to paddle frantically to keep up with her.

Trying to catch the four ducklings on the rock being called by their mother was like trying to catch four grasshoppers. Fortunately, the landing net proved to be equally effective on dry land: once I had 'em I had 'em.

By the time I had the six in the carton, Dora had made a couple of abortive attempts to lead the other two up over the oysters and finally had found enough sense to swim around the end of the rock and wade up the gradually sloping strip of sand between the rock and the cliff.

As soon as the ducklings were on the rock I grabbed them; they had no strength left to jump. Immediately, Dora flew at me and crash-landed on my head, where she scrambled around like an animated Melbourne Cup hat, wings flapping around my face, big webbed feet sliding all over my scalp. A ghastly sensation.

I hurled her off and she flew at me again, her wings brushing my shoulders as I ducked to avoid her stabbing beak. She turned and attacked a third time and a fourth, before landing on the roof of the duck house beside Charlie, who had leapt up there out of harm's way when I was racing around the rock slapping the net over his offspring. His contribution to the rescue operation had been to stand with his crest up hissing disapproval of the entire shooting match.

All three of us now agreed that the best place for the family until the brood was distributed among my duckling-loving friends, was back on the patch of land below the Dennises' house where Dora had successfully raised Charlie. It was above the level of the highest tides, sheltered from nearly all winds, and was familiar territory.

The ducklings adapted readily to their new home, Charlie didn't really care where he was so long as he was fed morning and night, and Dora seemed less nervy, less jumpy. With her brood around her, her whole demeanour reflected a sense of fulfilment.

I could count only five.

'Hey, Dora! Where are the other three?'

I guess it's difficult for a duck to register emotion. She just stared at me. She didn't look any different, but it was apparent that her sense of fulfilment had shriveled a little.

'Charlie! Where are the other three ducklings?'

He just stood on one foot and scratched his neck with the other.

I hunted all over the patch of land, crawling through the remaining lantana scrub, peering into holes in the ground and cracks between the rocks. I couldn't find even a whisk of yellow down. I walked along the foreshore. Not a sign. I couldn't tell who or what was to blame, the bush rats, a cat, the kookaburras. . .

And then there was one.

'Sure, we'll take it. We like nothing better than duckling, do we, Judy? By the way, how long will it be before it's ready? No point in keeping it till it's tough. . .

✳ ✳ ✳

115

"Thanks for the offer, but it's not worth the trouble today. All that business of plucking and cleaning. I'd just as soon buy one deep-frozen. . .'

So I picked up the duckling every afternoon, put it in a cardboard carton in the safety of the house for the night, and returned it to Dora in the morning.

This worked well initially, but understandably Dora found the arrangement less than satisfactory. I guess she didn't know whether she had a duckling or not. After a week or so she abandoned him entirely.

Indisputably, I was a better mother than Dora. Herb, as I called him because he had a black cap on his head like his father, was brought up strictly in accordance with the instructions in *Duck Raising*, with wet mash five times a day.

I found him an ideal home when he was still an adolescent. He slept in a box on the verandah, and during the day my friends' daughters dressed him in dolls' clothes, wheeled him around in a toy pram, and took him for swims in the goldfish pond. When he grew bigger and his feathers turned white, he was bathed weekly in the bath. When he was full grown his name was changed to Herbina.

He had laid an egg.

14

Deadbeats and scarlet women

I have a technique for catching things that hop, creep, crawl, fly inside the house when I'm sure that they really would be much happier outside. Things like grasshoppers, crickets, spiders, millipedes, bees, cicadas and other flying wazzits. The technique calls for strategy, patience and a sense of timing.

Clutching an empty jam jar or an upturned plastic ice-cream container in my right hand and a sheet of stiffish cardboard in my left, I stalk the creature until it lands on a clear flat surface then slap the jar or container over the top of it. Capture effected, I lift the container just a whisker on one side and slide the sheet of cardboard slowly underneath giving the creature time to do some fancy footwork and move on to the advancing cardboard. I then push my left hand under the cardboard and holding the container firmly against it, move into the great outdoors.

But when I saw the large black furry spider striding across the room my instincts served me well. I whipped off my shoe and swatted it.

I rang the museum. 'May I have the Spider Department?'

'I'll put you through to Arachnology.'

'Yes,' said the spider man, 'from your description I'd say it's a funnel-web. They're commonly found on the North Shore.'

'Are they really lethal?'

'Yes, they are. But I wouldn't worry too much. There have been relatively few recorded deaths since the country was settled.'

'That may be true, but I don't wish to be the next. I've never seen one inside before.'

'It's the wet weather we've been having. Your house is low to the ground?'

'Slap on it.'

'Then it's understandable. They live in burrows or tubes in the ground, shaded and often sheltered by litter, and also under rocks; breeding occurs during wet periods in summer and autumn when the males go in search of females.'

'Great. Every rainy spell I can expect to have a troop of sex-crazed funnel-webs moving in?'

'Not really, but you should be conscious of the possibility that one may occasionally come inside.'

Now I quite like spiders, but at this time I had not actually met a funnel-web face to face and was still somewhat under the influence of the remarkable folklore that has grown around the species. This has been compounded by an illustration of a monstrous black furry creature that could well have slipped in from outer space featured on the advertising hoardings of a pest-extermination firm exhorting householders to kill, kill, kill.

I dipped into that well of knowledge *The Australian Encyclopaedia*, to learn that of the 40 000 spider species known to exist worldwide, 1700 species are found in Australia, seventeen of which are harmful to humans. One, *Atrax robustus*, is considered to be one of the most deadly spiders on the face of the earth. Both male and female are poisonous, the male more so.

It was an *Atrax robustus* that I had clobbered with my shoe, presumably a male as it was on walkabout.

Over the years I've learned a little more about funnel-webs, and as someone who has led a bachelor existence for much of his life I have a certain compassion for the male of that species.

As I see it, the funnel-web world is not a man's world. Both males and females lead solitary lives in their silk-lined burrows which they make as immature spiders after leaving their mother's burrow. Having set up house they never leave it. The female can live there happily for seven or more years, a real stay-at-home.

In fact, neither male nor female funnel-webs go out hunting. They cleverly build trip lines of silk which radiate from the mouth of their burrow, forming an obstacle course for passing ants and other creeping and crawling creatures. When they feel peckish they go to the top of the burrow and lurk just below the surface with their feet or tips of their front legs over the edge. Sooner or later a creepy-crawly comes past, no doubt mumbling as it thrashes its way across the obstacle course, whereupon the funnel-web pounces.

This laid-back existence falls apart for the male come puberty at the age of two or so. From then on, except for a few brief moments if he's lucky, it's all downhill. In wet or humid weather in summer or autumn he ventures forth in search of someone he possibly has never seen as a grown-up—a lady funnel-web. Science is not quite sure how he recognises her, particularly as first contact is probably the sight of her feet clinging to the edge of her burrow. He's even been known to get stagefright once they've met on solid ground, leaping over her and scuttling off before they've been properly introduced. I can understand this as I have a friend who repeatedly acts in much the same way even though he is not in danger of being eaten by the object of his affection— which can be the lot of an unsuccessful funnel-web suitor.

Frankly, if I were a gentleman funnel-web I don't think I'd bother. I'd opt for the celibate life and retreat to a monastery, ideally Buddhist.

Having aroused the lady's interest by tapping on the silk she has spun at the entrance to her burrow and persuaded her to emerge, the male's main concern appears to be to keep out of the way of her fangs.

Copulation progresses, it seems to me, as a form of mixed-singles' spider wrestling, with the female rearing back in the strike position, the male blocking her fangs by pressing against her forelegs with his, while hooking spurs on his second legs around her second legs.

After accepting her lover's sperm the female retires to her burrow and hangs up a pillow-shaped cocoon of fertilised eggs like a bunch of garlic in a French provincial kitchen.

Away from his own burrow, the male leads the life of a deadbeat wandering from one spot to another, dossing down under wet rocks or scraps of wood or old sheets of galvanised iron, scarcely eating, becoming dehydrated and, being out in the open for much of the time, fair game for predators. The life span after initial copulation—there may be other joyous occasions—can be less, much less, than nine months.

And there are *those* women, snug in their burrows. . .

Part of the folklore about funnel-webs is that they are credited with amazing agility. Few people would be aware that a lovesick young funnel-web can have a fit of nerves at the last minute and leap over the lady he has been pursuing, but countless first-hand observers are prepared to swear that they have seen a funnel-web jump a metre, even two. I've actually heard it maintained that when attacking human beings a funnel-web unfailingly goes for the jugular.

I now know that arachnologists, that is, spider people, poo-hoo the idea of giant leaps. Sure, a funnel-web can jump a centimetre or so they say, but stop worrying about your jugular.

However, it's only commonsense to be wary in areas where funnel-webs are found. Along with the rest of the populace in funnel-web territory I tend to upend boots and shoes and give them a good thumping before putting them on, and usually wear thick gloves when working outdoors. I have yet to find a funnel-web in a shoe but I've encountered many a one in the garden.

In my early years in the bay, I leant towards the live-and-let-live principle unless I found them in a spot where they could be a danger. Once, when I was levering a sizable piece of sandstone from a bank I revealed a funnel-web at the bottom of its silk-lined burrow, rather like a child's ant house built in a box with one glass wall. Exposed to the world, the funnel-web cringed: I retain an image of it with its front legs before its eyes like a heroine in peril in a Victorian melodrama. I apologised for the intrusion and put the slab of sandstone back.

Huh? And the creature's lethal? Well, yes, but I thought it was in an out-of-the-way area of the garden where it would do no one any harm. I was prepared to take what I considered was the slight risk of it going walkabout in my direction. Somehow, I felt that to destroy its burrow would be the act of a vandal. This was some years ago. Today, I'd be more inclined to whip off my shoe and swat it.

Unquestionably, funnel-web spiders can and do kill. Since my first inquiry the death roll has gone up to thirteen, and the lives of a number of other spider-bite victims have been saved by treatment with an antivenene.

I believe that the female victim who was the subject of a news item on the Australian Broadcasting Corporation's radio network some years ago was one of those who has survived, but she possibly is still explaining just what did happen to her. The usually smoothly articulate newsreader got flummoxed and read: 'Mrs Dorothy Aitken of Blacktown was bitten on the funnel by a finger-webbed spider'.

A bite from a funnel-web is by no means a death sentence. A friend was once a nurse at a major hospital in funnel-web territory. Repeatedly, at weekends, a white-faced individual in gardening clothes would be rushed into Casualty by someone clutching a bucket with the remains of a funnel-web spider squashed flat for being foolish enough to bite a human being. Invariably, the victim recovered without drastic treatment but the medical staff kept close watch, ever at the ready to administer the antivenene. Only a fool would take the bite of a funnel-web lightly.

Martha sat on my desk throughout each day. She was, I have to admit, a scarlet woman, heavily rouged in a most unlikely place. She had an appalling reputation, but with me her manners were perfect. A kept woman, she nevertheless had a strong domestic streak and had set up house, constantly adding to the living area, adjusting the decorations and the furnishings at frequent intervals in an almost finicky way.

I actually met her strolling along my desk and was immediately curious about her. Certainly her looks attracted me: she was petite with long slim legs, but I was most intrigued by that appalling reputation. I just had to possess her. Martha was a red-back spider.

To catch Martha I selected a medium-sized pickle jar and, approaching from the side opposite my shadow, dropped it neatly around her. It was a breeze. Having slid in the cardboard and pushed my hand under it, I slowly tilted the jar, pressing very hard against the cardboard. For some time she was reluctant to accept that the world was turning upside down and clung there. So I gave the jar a little tap on the desk and she slid gracefully down the glass to the bottom. I then stretched a double layer of plastic wrap across the top and secured it further with an elastic band. For ventilation, I jabbed the plastic wrap a number of times with the tip of a fine-bladed knife.

More or less in a reflex action, I reached for the encyclopaedia and turned to 'Spiders (Araneae), an order of the Arachnida, a class that also includes ticks, mites, scorpions and Opiliones or harvestmen'.

Now that was of immediate interest. I had skipped over the preliminaries when looking up funnel-webs some time before and until now had not realised that ticks, which abound in our neck of the woods during the summer months and can be fatal to pets and can paralyse human beings, are actually related to spiders. I was within a whisker of turning to the Superphosphate-to-Zygophyllaceae volume where I was bound to find 'Ticks' but restrained myself. The opening of an encyclopaedia has been the root cause of many a wasted hour thinly disguised as broadening my knowledge. I am led relentlessly on from one fascinating bit of information to the next until I have forgotten entirely what it was that caused me to pick up the book in the first place.

My willpower was assisted by a sentence that jumped out at me: 'Mice are occasionally caught, killed and eaten by red-back spiders. . .'

I stared incredulously at the spider in the jar. But you're the size of a pea! Martha—I have no explanation as to why she instantly became Martha—can you really wrestle a mouse to the ground? This must be the equivalent of a possum annihilating a rhinoceros.

The punch line was at the end. 'The only native species which have been responsible for deaths [in Australia] are *Latrodectus mactans* and *Atrax robustus*. . .' The deaths referred to weren't those of mice: they were those of humans beings.

Atrax robustus were my old friends the funnel-webs; *Latrodectus mactans* were, yes, Marthas.

So here I was sharing this idyllic situation with the world's deadliest spider and another that seemed to come a close second.

I read on: '. . .The red-back is shining black with a red streak above and a red hour-glass pattern below the abdomen. . .' No question about what Martha was. '. . .The spider is a geographic variant of the widely distributed *Latrodectus mactans*, a species which includes the black widow of America and the katipo of New Zealand. . .[The Australian variant is actually known as *Latrodectus hasseltii*; the New Zealand variant as *Latrodectus katipo* or, commonly, night stinger.]. . .deaths have resulted from red-back spider bite. However, since the development of an effective antivenene in the 1950s the seriousness of the red-back spider bite has diminished. Administration of the antivenene considerably allays the symptoms of abdominal and lower limb pains and the profuse sweating which if untreated may continue for several days. . .'

Great! I ran my eye over the text again. I'd missed a bit. '. . .In unsewered areas it has always been a hazard in privies because of its liking for dark, sheltered and confined sites. . .'

Here was food for thought. I looked closely at Martha in the jar, wondering if I should be feeling a tinge of embarrassment. How well *did* she know me? Was she a resident of the small stained-glass-windowed house on the hillside who had been in a position to 'run her eye over me', so to speak, on more than one occcasion? And if so, what was the saucy hussy doing on my desk? In more ways than one it was somewhat disquietening.

Leaving Martha in the jar I got a torch and walked up the hill where I lifted the lid of the amenity and made a thorough inspection. To my relief there was no sign of red-back habitation: many an Australian country town has a not-so-funny story or two to tell about how Fred or Susie was bitten by a red-back on the you-know-where. To be on the safe side, I pushed ecological values to one side and gave the amenity a thorough going over with a strong insect spray.

My intention had been to find out more about Martha and spiders in general then release her in the bush a long way from home. At least I think it was, but somehow day succeeded day and Martha remained in the jar on my desk. Okay, so I have double standards. I can't bear to see birds in small cages but here I was with a sweet little *Latrodectus hasseltii* cooped up in a jar.

I think I was intrigued by the domesticity bit. She seemed to have been with me only five minutes when she started spinning a web in the bottom of the jar. Admittedly, it was a scruffy little web but at least she was trying. Martha seemed to me like a new bride who had been spoiled rotten by her mother and had never done a tap of housework in her life.

On the evening of the first day, having fed Dora, Charlie and Blossom Richardson I heard a mosquito buzzing around my head and deftly ended the nuisance raid by slapping it between the palms of both hands. Ah, I thought, Martha's supper. I laid the corpse on the plastic wrap stretched across the top of the jar and pushed it through one of the air holes with the point of the slim-bladed knife. (I still found it difficult to believe that bit about red-backs consuming mice.) Later, when I looked at the jar, Martha appeared to be sitting on the mosquito.

So I got the fly swat out of a kitchen cupboard and put it on my desk. Thenceforth, Martha was regularly fed partially squashed flies, mosquitoes, ants and various unidentified creatures.

I thought our relationship was entirely satisfactory although it did seem to concern visitors to the cottage. I never did get around to taking her for a ride to distant bush: she seemed to fit in well and just became part of the scene.

Then one afternoon I returned from a visit to the city and after saying hello to Blossom Richardson, who somehow had taken to stretching out on the sofa, called a cheery greeting to Martha.

I didn't really expect a response, but glancing at the jar I could see only her very messy web and a couple of demised, unconsumed flies.

I looked more closely.

No Martha.

I stood back a metre or so and looked around the desk.

Nary a sign.

How could she have climbed the slippery sides of the jar which she must have equated with an ice wall on the face of Mont Blanc, worked her way across the plastic wrap upside down, and crawled out through a ventilation slit a fraction the size of her body?

Sufficient to say the strength of a determined woman who has had enough of an unsatisfactory situation can move mountains. I had sense enough to realise that the relationship had been entirely one-sided.

So there I was in my office area surrounded by stacks of manila folders containing several reams of paper and boxes of pencils, pens, pins, slide clips, rubber bands and the like— and somewhere a lurking, probably disgruntled female *Latrodectus hasseltii*.

I pulled on a pair of leather-palmed gardening gloves and started. Over some hours I sifted through every scrap of paper, every receptacle. I examined the curtains, cupboards, corners.

The mystery of Martha's disappearance remains unsolved to this day.

Several years passed before I again had a female *Latrodectus hasseltii* as a guest on my desk. She had come all the way from the shores of Lake Frome, a semi-arid region in northeastern South Australia.

I had been there with an American palaeontologist gathering material for a story about the scientific search for the origins of Australia's unique marsupials—the kangaroo, koala, wombat and so on. A fascinating subject that, like Martha's disappearance, is still unexplained.

We had only just arrived in the area where the scientist had been digging on his last trip and had left my 4WD utility truck to search for a low cairn he had built to enable him to find the precise site of the dig in the flat, near-featureless landscape. We walked for a kilometre or so, following a dry creek bed, before we found the cairn which was a pile of small rocks less than a metre high. As we stood talking I noticed that a rock had fallen off the top, and being of a tidy mind I picked it up with my left hand and replaced it. Lifting the rock from the ground I felt a sharp sting in my thumb and thought I must have picked up a burr with the rock. My thumb continued to sting then throb and I thought, maybe I've been stung by a bull ant. Curious, I lifted an edge of the rock—and there was a chubby little scarlet woman, a *Latrodectus hasseltii*.

I realise this should be the prelude to a wild dash along rough tracks to the nearest homestead; a radio call to the Flying Doctor; gripping pains; and so on.

I feel a fraud. Apart from the sting, I felt absolutely nothing.

We stood there for a minute or two, me holding my arm high and gripping my wrist firmly to inhibit the blood flow, one half of my mind saying, 'You are calm. . . You are very calm. . .', the other half trying to recall the precise details of what I had read about red-back bites. Most clearly I remembered that they were sudden death on mice but immediately countered this thought by doing some rapid mental arithmetic on relative body weights.

'How are you feeling?' asked the palaeontologist anxiously.

I shrugged—minimally. 'No different from usual.' I was keeping very still, wondering whether it would be best for me to lie down where I was and have him go back for the truck or ask him to carry me to it. Neither alternative appealed. With the former, if I passed out he could well have difficulty finding me again in the flat, featureless landscape (it had taken a while to locate the low cairn in the first place); with the latter, it struck me that the effect on my bloodstream could be that of vigorously shaking a cocktail, which would create the opposite of the desired effect.

'I think we should walk back to the truck quite slowly,' I said, which we did.

I sat quietly in the front seat of the 4WD for another half hour or so feeling no sensation whatsoever apart from my throbbing thumb. All of this seemed a waste of an expedition that had taken weeks to organise, so I suggested to the palaeontologist that he drive the truck back to the site and get on with his dig.

He didn't seem too happy about my next suggestion that he catch the spider in case I had a turn for the worse and it was needed for identification by a doctor. But he did so.

Which was how another *Latrodectus hasseltii* came to be sitting in a jar on my desk.

I checked with the museum arachnologist. Yep, it was a female red-back, and it's the female that's deadly.

'How deadly?' I asked.

'Well, the number of recorded deaths is now up to sixteen. A red-back can kill a baby, even a child, but it's unlikely to kill a *healthy* adult. Mind you, anyone bitten can be awfully ill.'

'But I had no reaction, none whatsoever?'

'Oh?' said the arachnologist. 'Maybe it didn't bite you properly: they have quite small fangs.'

'It seemed to hang on all the way from the ground to the top of the cairn.'

'Maybe it had just eaten and so had expended its venom.'

'It seemed to be sitting at home under its rock; it wasn't out hunting.'

'Well, maybe you're one of the lucky ones who are more resistant to red-back venom.'

'Living where I do that would be an extremely fortunate attribute. How about funnel-webs?'

He laughed. 'I wouldn't push my luck.'

But I like to think that maybe there's a link here with the lion-with-a-thorn-in-its-foot story. Maybe the word has got around the spider world that I could have pulped Martha, but instead set her up in a luxury, glass-walled apartment and plied her with the finest cuisine.

I only hope I haven't compounded the spider problem in the Sydney area. Her Lake Frome sister is out there some-where.

15

The price of summer

The windows and outside doors were shut and the curtains were drawn to blot out the heat. The strong wind that blew from the northwest across the harbour brought no relief, only powdery grey snow that was not snow but fine ash.

The northwest sky and the sky to the north and to the northeast were grey with smoke, the grey shading from off-white through to near-black and stabbed at intervals with shafts of orange and red.

One of the several fires burning on the skyline was just beyond the hump of the ridge on the far shore. It was hidden from my view, but I could visualise it moving swiftly along the steep, thickly treed face of the western shore of Roseville Chase, the flames gulping the undergrowth, leaping from treetop to treetop driven hard by the wind.

I looked uneasily at the near-identical shoreline extending from the head of our bay to the point opposite the ridge on the far shore. There was a pocket of houses on the hillside near the point and a scattering of houses above the bay.

Jock had told me that once flame or wind-borne cinders had been carried across the harbour, here some hundreds of metres wide, and started fires in the bush on the point. Fortunately, there were men on the spot and the fires were beaten out before they could take hold.

The conditions on this day were identical: intense summer heat, the existence of thick undergrowth promoted by a succession of good seasons, and a strong northwesterly wind.

If it had happened before, it could happen again, and there may not be men on the spot. If fire did take hold. . .

Smoke billowed to the north, south and west of Sydney. Fire was the price all too often paid for the areas of bushland, reserves and national parks that enrich the city.

A similar price is paid repeatedly summer after summer in many parts of Australia, and the horror of it will never go away.

My unease increased as the sky darkened further and the hot wind strengthened. I went outside, checked that the hose was connected to the garden tap and was free of knots and kinks, and got several empty cornsacks from under the cottage, the countryman's fire beaters.

I glanced up at the gutters edging the roof, a danger point in a bushfire, but I knew they were safe; I had taken the precaution of clearing them of leaves only a day or so before, and had plugged the downpipes with tennis balls and filled the gutters with water. However, the tar-impregnated malthoid covering of the near-flat, skillion roof on three sides would be seriously at risk if red-hot ashes were flying.

Looking at the trees and scrub so close in the reserve at the head of the bay, I wondered what the effect would be if fire did leap the gap and race along the hillside. The conformation of the hills above the bay played strange tricks with wind. I had long ago given up sailing on to my mooring: I could be moving gently into a head wind, timing it perfectly to pick up the buoy when suddenly wind could come from astern and I would be hurtling towards the shore.

The only sound was the hot wind in the trees. No birds called; the cicadas, which earlier had been drumming with ear-aching intensity, were silent.

I returned to my desk and was making a pretence of working when I glanced up to see the humped ridge on the opposite shore suddenly glow red along its entire length, and as I watched flame seemed to spill over as lava spews down the sides of a volcano.

The speed and the sense of menace of advancing, wind-driven fire never fails to thud in the gut. I hurried outside and by the time I reached the hose the line of flame was a third the way down the far hillside.

I turned the tap on full and began drenching the house, the malthoid roof, and the surrounding grass, shrubs and trees.

The fall of grey ash thickened. Looking directly at the flames swallowing the far hillside at alarming speed the heat of the wind seemed intensified.

Then as I watched, ripples appeared on the surface of the water. I looked to the south. White horses were rushing up the harbour, faster and faster, growing higher and higher, thrust forward by the solid force of the wind that Sydney gaspingly awaits in late-afternoon, midsummer heat, the Southerly Buster.

Boats plunged on their moorings, trees bowed to the north, the waters of the harbour churned.

And as the flames enveloped the foreshore, great red and orange tongues licking out over the rocks, the Buster slammed against them, driving them back, back against the already wasted hillside.

Within fewer minutes than it had taken for the fire to rush down from the ridge it was no more.

'I'll be damned!' I muttered. 'That's the sort of thing desperate men have prayed for on their knees before being burned to a frazzle. And I've seen it happen.'

I turned off the hose and stood staring at the far shore and the scattering of small fires burning harmlessly in isolation on the blackened hillside.

'You've been lucky again, old timer,' I said to the cottage as I walked back inside. Then I thought of the people beneath the smoke on the skyline and could sense the awful desperation of those who stood in the ashes of what an hour or so before had been their home.

16

Three leaps sideways

Every three or four years my life seems to leap sideways. No leap has been planned, at least not by me. At such times I liken myself to a weird insect I once watched for the better part of an hour. It had an orange-coloured, oval-shaped body and a glossy black head to which were appended eyes on sticks, an elephant's trunk and a pair of extraordinarily long feelers. It moved deliberately along a bush track on its many legs, seemingly with a sense of purpose, then without warning it would leap sideways, land squarely on its feet and continue walking in a different direction with the same uncompromising sense of purpose.

To me, it was an extremely exciting insect. Repeatedly, the new direction was not for the better in that the insect found itself thrashing through clumps of grass that towered over its body, clambering over twigs that must have seemed like giant fallen trees, and scrambling up and over pebbles that it must have equated with monolothic Uluru in central Australia.

Even so, I felt I understood what it was on about. It could have kept on walking straight ahead down the cleared, well-worn bush path where I first saw it. But that would have been all that it was doing—walking down a well-worn path. The sudden leap, seemingly prompted by a brain spasm, gave it a totally new sense of direction, a new sense of purpose. Had I been a scientist I would have named my discovery *Leaperosis fraserae* or whatever the scientific term is for sideways-leaping creatures.

Leaperosis fraserae came back to mind when in three sideways leaps I suddenly found myself behind a desk in a publishing house. . .at the altar. . .and up the hill.

Everything was different. I was a city gent in a pinstripe suit with corporate responsibilities, I had a corporate wife from within the organisation, and I had an almost conventional house.

As an operation, the last of the three could not have been easier. Squire Wilcox had subdivided his land and built a new house at road level and I took a lease on his old house that was only halfway down—or up—the hillside, level with my friends the Muirs.

It might seem extreme to maintain that there was a difference over a distance of fifty metres, but there was. It was something I had casually observed many times before but it was driven home now. There were differences when you moved up or down the hillside, to one side or the other; differences in aspect, differences in the character of the surroundings.

Life in the cottage on the waterfront was, in some ways, like living aboard a boat. Three sides of the house were comprised of windows, so that whenever I looked out I saw water. I remained attuned to the water the way I had been over the years prior to moving to the bay when I was running a boat business and spending half my life actually on the water. I was conscious of changes in the weather, shifts of wind, the run of the tide.

And the sounds were related to the water: the soft swish and gentle lapping in calm weather disturbed only by the surge and brief turbulence created by the wash of a passing boat; the ceaseless crashing of waves against the rocks during a storm. And in my early days there, when the majority of boats were still made of timber, day and night the soft slap, slap, slap of running rigging against wooden masts, changing over time to the sharper tap, tap, tap of stainless-steel wire striking aluminium.

The birds I saw and heard—or at least was most conscious of—were principally water birds. Seagulls dominated the air above the harbour and the shoreline. Their numbers varied at different times from a mere scattering to flocks of birds feeding on seething schools of small fish. They would perch on the posts at the end of the jetty and, to the chagrin of every boat owner, on the masts and decks of the growing number of yachts and motor cruisers in the bay raucously arguing for possession of a favoured spot.

Occasionally, a few terns would join them, their fine-tuned diving bodies, black heads and long beaks catching the eye. Rarely, a pelican would happen by, its presence in this deep-water area of the harbour to be wondered at, pondered upon. More frequently, sea eagles would wheel high in the sky.

At almost any time, cormorants could be seen diving for fish or standing on a rock or branch drying their outstretched wings, while a white-faced heron or two waded in the shallows with infinite grace or stood elegantly on the shore, grey bodies blending with the background.

As a special treat, every now and then an azure kingfisher would fly from tree to tree and even perch on one of the jetty posts, staring into the water for long periods with remarkable patience and concentration giving me time to marvel at its glorious dominant blue colouring.

Looking down from one of the front windows I would watch fish swimming close in on a high tide. After being fished by Europeans for two centuries, Sydney Harbour today is not really rich in fish but there are times when the catch is quite good. Bream are found throughout the year, but in the summer, when feed is plentiful, the big silver bream come in from the ocean as well as kingfish and trevally; in winter, tailor can be seen pursuing schools of smaller fish which break the surface of the water in their bid to escape, only to encounter opportunistic seagulls screeching overhead.

It's probably fantasy, but I became convinced that the same compact school of large bream came into the bay year after year. Looking down, I would see flashes of silver in the light of the morning sun as they weaved gracefully in and out of the jetty piles and I believed I recognised this one and that from the year before.

I didn't fish from the jetty any more.

Up the hillside, at road level, there was not that same link with the water. The views were magnificent, broad and sweeping. But there was not a feeling of being at one with the harbour. It was there to be stared at, admired. At road level you were conscious of passing traffic, light though it was. On the waterfront, or even halfway down the hillside, the motor car might not have existed.

So I now found myself living not, in effect, on the deck of a boat but at the masthead. The water, and the increasing number of yachts and motor cruisers on their moorings, were below me. The harbour was still there, but I no longer felt part of it. When I turned my head a little to either side I looked into the foliage of trees.

The new house was an architecturally unpretentious rectangular box with fairly modern amenities and, like the cottage, windowed right across the front. It was three times the size of the cottage, but comfortable and friendly, and the unobscured view was superb.

All of this was fine; it was simply different. Even the birds were different.

In the four years I had lived there, I had not fully appreciated the richness of the birdlife of the bay. I had been looking at water birds with my back to the birds on the wooded hillside above me. Now, as the dominant raucous cries of the seagulls gave way to the wonderfully distinctive calls of magpies, butcherbirds, currawongs and kookaburras, I became more aware of the diversity of species.

Families of noisy miners chatted endlessly as they searched for insects and sipped nectar in the trees and shrubs, and at frequent intervals banded together to harass intruders many times their size such as honey-eating wattle birds, even a pair of whistling kites.

From the pocket of rainforest at the head of the bay came the whipcrack-like call of the whipbird, closely followed by the 'choo-choo' response of his mate. In spring and summer,

black-faced cuckoo shrikes rolled *chereer-chereer* and dollar birds gave their harsh *cak-cak* call as they tumbled in the late-afternoon sky catching insects on the wing, and koels and pallid cuckoos gave their repetitive renditions of the ever-ascending scale. At night, came the soft *oomp, oomp, oomp* of the tawny frogmouth and the harsher *mo-poke, mo-poke* of the boobook.

Most notable perhaps were the superb members of the parrot family—flocks of rainbow lorikeets splashed with the colours of a painter's palette, engaging, gregarious birds that would swoop down in their dozens calling for sweetened bread that sadly is as bad for them as handfuls of chocolates are for children; and strikingly marked rosellas, both the eastern and crimson species, that invariably came in pairs; and larrikin, sulphur-crested cockatoos with their extrovert cries which visited singly and in flocks.

For many of the birds, the halfway mark on the hillside was their flight path as they moved around the bay, and my workroom in a front corner of the new house proved to be an admirable viewing platform for the birds that flashed past or landed in the adjacent tall trees.

That is, when I was at home to observe them.

The leap sideways that had propelled me into the corporate

world landed me in an office grandly described as a 'suite'. There was my office proper with a vast desk and a vast swivel chair opening off another office with desks for a secretary and editorial assistants. This adjoined a conference room with a very long table and a lot of chairs. I had been lured there by interesting and challenging work, producing big-budget books that I believed were worthwhile—and bags of gold. In my years of writing no one had offered me bags of gold before. The catch was that they were more a dowry: I was expected to 'marry' the organisation. At least, that's the way it seemed to me.

I must have got carried away by this marrying concept because in time I found myself tying the knot, as they say, with the head of the research department.

Working with Margot on publishing projects was great. She was a brilliant editorial researcher with a lively, far-reaching mind, who had considerable knowledge of Australia's fauna and flora. Naturally, the birds in the area were a joy to her, as were the other creatures of the bay; the possums, echidnas, bandicoots, things that crept and crawled, the ducks, Rummy the dingo and Blossom Richardson. After long working days in the city fielding problems that are an integral part of the publishing business, the house on the hillside became for both of us a valued haven.

Rummy, I believe, found the new address extremely convenient: he had only to stroll next door for a chat and an ear scratch. Blossom Richardson also found it satisfactory, proving this by choosing to have a batch of kittens in the wardrobe. We still called her Blossom Richardson even though she had long since packed her bags and left the Richardson home. When I moved up the hill she had simply followed.

But the new situation was not conducive to duck raising. An old friend, who by coincidence had also recently married, had moved into the cottage on the waterfront and Squire Wilcox had converted a detached storeroom at the rear of the cottage into a comfortable bedroom. To feed the ducks entailed tripping past the bridal chamber, which I was disinclined to do. I dashed off for an early start at the office in the morning, and I was often bumbling around in the dark in the evening.

It may not come as a surprise to learn that I had found duck raising on a rock in Middle Harbour charged with drama. True, by persistence, analysis, lateral thinking, manual labour and the expenditure of an inordinate amount of time, I had overcome the major problem of security as clutch succeeded clutch. I enclosed the open patio attached to the duck house with a rat-proof, possum-proof, cat-proof wire cage, forming quite spacious quarters that both Dora and each new batch of ducklings accepted as home.

Every morning, I would open the door leading to the ramp, the ducklings would rush down and Dora would follow more sedately. In the afternoon, I got them back into the cage simply by putting a tray of mash on the patio and the ducklings would rush back up the ramp, again followed by Dora, whereupon the door was slammed shut. As I have said, the duck house was home.

By good fortune I had come across a delightful couple with a young family who were living the good life in a rural setting on the outskirts of the city and were happy to take each brood when the ducklings were half-grown.

However, I must admit that drama was never far away when the ducklings were *out*, and I could scarcely expect my friend and his young wife to devote their lives to duckling-rescue operations.

Dora and Charlie had become a real problem. Reluctantly, we decided that finally, irrevocably, they would have to go. But where?

I was pondering on this early one morning as I went up the path to collect the milk. A note was propped against the bottle, scrawled on the back of a promotional leaflet extolling the virtues of yoghurt. It read:

> Stop patting the ducks o literary one,
> Sit down and write that cheque.
> I'm going broke for want of cash
> So do your best by heck.
>
> (Sgd) Joe Shakedough

Joe had a way with his reminder notices for overdue accounts. Not really material to make up a slim volume, but as a memory jogger his doggerel had the desired effect.

It also reminded me that Joe, who was not your run-of-the-mill milkman, being an engineering tradesman of some sort with the milk-delivery run a second string to his bow, lived on a farmlet in the area where I had purchased the duckling Charlotte. As I was at the end of his round, we had many a chat when I met him on my morning walk and he had described his property, of which he was very proud, in glowing terms. I had an image of rolling lawns and lily ponds which, it suddenly occurred to me, could only be enhanced by the presence of water fowl.

The next morning I was waiting for Joe, cash in hand.

Sure, he'd take over Dora and Charlie. His children had read a story I had written about them and he felt sure they would love to care for the hero and heroine. He already had a few ducks so they would have company. He'd discuss the matter with his family and let me know.

Propped against a milk bottle the next day:

> Saturday arvo you may call
> Bring Dora, Charlie, your wife and all.
> A social drink we'll have together,
> Let's hope it's not inclement weather.

I doubt that Charlie had a sense of homecoming. He was in a corn sack on the back floor of the car all fluffed up with indignation. Dora was beside him in another sack, even more outraged.

We turned left off the road that led to Charlie's place of birth—or should it be hatching?—following another dirt track. Joe and his excited children were waiting at the open gate. He gave a wave and signalled for us to follow. We drove into a paddock and Joe walked ahead up the slope. Looking around as we crawled behind him in low gear we could see no sign of rolling lawns or lily ponds.

Joe stopped at a wire-netting fowl yard. He indicated the entrance with a grand gesture. 'They'll be fine in here,' he said.

My mind was flipping through rhetoric of travel brochures.

Lily ponds? There weren't even water glimpses! It was very depressing.

Joe's children were jumping up and down excitedly.

Don't be ridiculous, I reminded myself. They're only ducks. And you're committed.

'See,' Joe said. 'They'll be able to splash around in there.' He pointed to a muddied hole in the fowl yard half-full of water. It wasn't Sydney Harbour.

I picked up the sack containing Charlie, carried it into the fowl yard and put it on the ground. The children were already untying the string that closed the sack.

Charlie staggered out, shook himself to rearrange his feathers, then spotted several ducks among the chickens. Immediately, Old Macho strode across the run, scattering the chickens, and proceeded to prove his manhood to the nearest duck.

Joe stared at him admiringly, hands on hips. 'Now, there's a *breeder!*' he said.

'Where's Dora?' the children were clamouring.

This could be the best thing for her, I rationalised. She *needs* another half dozen ducks, female ducks that is, around to take the pressure off. Go get her.

I brought her from the car, opened the sack, and she shot out, neck stretched, beady eyes darting in all directions assessing the situation.

Three of the ducks not occupied with Charlie waddled over and promptly set about establishing the pecking order.

'Hey!' Joe shouted. 'Easy on!' He kicked the three ducks out of the way but they immediately circled back intent on reinforcing precedence. Joe scratched his head. 'Guess they'll have to sort things out for themselves. The life Dora's been leading she should be able to look after herself.'

But she was again pounced on by the other three who lashed at her with their beaks and it was very clear where she was going to stand in the order of things. She sought refuge in the muddy pool.

I looked around the fowl yard, uncertain of what to do, while Joe proudly pointed out the features of the establishment. As a rough old bush fowl yard I guess it was okay, but I know my dad would have been in there tidying up with a rake and filling the tins with fresh water.

Charlie was preening his feathers and eyeing off another duck; he found nothing wrong with the place at all. Dora was treading water in the pool, wings twitching. I knew the signs. I was afraid that she would suddenly take off and garrotte herself in the wire netting.

Bloody Joe, I was thinking. This isn't what I had in mind.

Relax, I reminded myself. You should have known he was kidding about the rolling lawns and lily ponds fronting the manor house. He's always pulling your leg.

I know, I know. Joe's an English migrant and I guess what he has now seems like a grand estate by comparison with the Midlands terrace house he left behind. But I had expected at least a grassy paddock, an earth dam—and space. Dora in a *fowl yard!*

We declined an invitation to tea pleading pressing business and drove back down the dirt track. Clear of the farmlet, I found the car going slower and slower. Neither of us spoke. Then Margot said, 'We can't leave Dora there.'

'That's what I've been thinking. But how can we tell Joe that? He obviously sees his little patch as the Antipodean Garden of Eden.'

'I guess he does.' Dully.

We continued to crawl along the track. 'Well,' I sighed, 'at least Charlie will be happy. He only ever sits around nowadays. All he seems to want is his dinner and sex.' And warming to my rationalisation, 'He really was too demanding of Dora. Now he's got a harem, which is as it should be. How many ducks does *Duck Raising* say there should be for every drake?'

'I'm sorry, but I've never read *Duck Raising*,' she said absently. Which would have been the only book I'd ever mentioned that she hadn't read. Then she said thoughtfully, 'I wonder if the Dennises would feed her?'

We called down. Yes, of course they would, said Lorna and Ross. They would put a bowl of fresh water on the concrete landing under their cottage and feed her there. She would soon get used to the change. Besides, the girls were most upset when they saw us taking them away.

I restrained myself until next morning, then rang Joe. The little girls next door were devastated, I told him, and had cried half the night. They wanted Dora back.

Joe laughed. He understood. He'd explain the situation to his own youngsters.

We were there with the chaff bag in half an hour and Dora almost jumped into it.

Charlie was engaged with another duck and didn't even bother to look up.

We put Dora back on her rock and she immediately took off, did a circuit of the bay, then landed on the sandflat where she began foraging. She was home.

'It's a puzzle,' said Joe shaking his head and sorting through his milk bottles to cover his embarrassment. 'He just disappeared. One minute he was there, the next he was gone. We've looked everywhere, around the house, in the bush. . .We even went over to the poultry farm next door where they've got ducks, but there seemed to be a dozen Charlies. I couldn't tell one from the other.' He looked at me hopefully. 'We were wondering if maybe he took off and headed for the harbour.'

'Like a homing pigeon?'

'You said he was a pretty good flier.'

'Only short range. And I wouldn't bet on his intelligence to master the navigation.'

We never did find out what happened to Charlie, but I like to think that he became airborne and made it as far as the poultry farm and was one of the dozen 'Charlies' Joe saw. If so, he would have had a harem beyond his wildest dreams and unquestionably would have led a long and fruitful life.

That's if the poultry farmer knew a good breeder when he saw one.

17

A little lulu

'But they'll kill it,' said Margot.

I put a foot on the edge of my vast office desk and pushed so that I rocked back in my vast swivel chair. 'No they won't: they're in business.'

'No one will buy the poor little thing.' She put a bunch of spinach on my desk and leaned forward, earnest, concerned. 'It's really, well, it's got this mad little face, black on one side and orange—a beautiful orange—on the other side.'

'Sounds great. All we need is a schizoid cat.' And my eyes drifted to the pile of proofs on my desk hollering for attention.

But Margot didn't give up easily. 'No, it's really sweet; it's special. All it needs is a little ointment and I'm sure its eye will be right in a day or two.'

'What? You mean we'd be up for vet bills before we even started!'

'It's only a minor thing. Didn't Blossom Richardson have a sore eye that took no time at all to heal?'

'At great expense.'

'I'll pay for the ointment. Listen, it will only be for a few days until its eye gets better, and I'm sure its whiskers will straighten out once it gets some decent food.'

'Its whiskers will what?'

'Straighten. Some of them are a bit bent; but it makes her look quite engaging.'

'Her?'

'Yes, it's a female. But really, I'll find a home for her as soon as she's looking her best. We won't have the expense of getting her spayed.'

'Margot, today is Friday. I *know* it's Friday because Friday is Paddy's Market Day and you've got an armful of fruit and veg. On Monday, just last Monday, I had to steel myself to dispose of four of Blossom Richardson's latest batch of kittens because we couldn't find homes for them. Remember? We're in the middle of a national kitten glut.'

She added a bag of bananas and half a butternut pumpkin to the spinach on my desk and said defiantly, 'They were all funny. You said yourself something was wrong with them and that maybe Blossom Richardson shouldn't have any more kittens.'

'So you pick this little lulu—a schizoid, two-tone-faced cat with a bung eye and broken whiskers.'

She looked at me steadily across the vast desk for a second or two, then said sadly, 'No one will buy it; they'll kill it'.

The hardened disposer of kittens crumbled. 'Okay, so long as you really do find a home for it. Your job, not mine.'

Margot was petite, fast moving. She was out the door and down the corridor to her office where she dumped the fruit and veg and was back to the pet stall in Paddy's Market in a shot.

I emerged from my office a little later when I heard oohing and aahing and considerable laughter along the corridor. A strange little creature, just as Margot had described, with a patchy tortoiseshell coat and disproportionately large paws, was exploring the carpet. It couldn't have been more than four weeks old.

'What are you going to call it?' someone asked.

'Nothing,' I said from the doorway, 'it's in transit.'

I was ignored. The staff knew a hardened disposer of kittens when they saw one.

'Cumquat,' said another. 'I just bought some at the markets to make marmalade. Those orangey patches actually are the colour of a cumquat.'

'If you're expecting your other cat to adopt it,' said a third in leaden tones, 'forget it. A mother cat won't have a bar of other kittens. She could kill it.'

It seemed that whichever way this cat jumped it faced a sticky end.

We were going out to dinner that evening. It was after one o'clock when we said goodnight to our host and hostess. The cumquat-coloured, two-tone-faced, in-transit kitten was contentedly asleep in a cardboard carton in the car.

Blossom Richardson was sitting on the far side of the living room when we entered. Tentatively, Margot put the kitten down, ready to snatch it up should Blossom attack. The kitten spotted Blossom and galloped towards her. Blossom looked at the kitten in surprise then flopped down and lay on her side. The action was spontaneous: she was still in milk. The kitten pounced on her and in seconds was suckling contentedly, her big paws kneading Blossom's silver-grey fur.

Within a couple of days the bung eye popped open, the bent whiskers twanged straight. Weeks went by; the question of finding a home was never raised. It seemed we had another cat.

Thus began a wonderful mother–daughter relationship. The two were inseparable and never grew out of the habit of curling up together to sleep when they would form remarkably varied entwined patterns. Doubtless the relationship remained unchanged because we had Blossom spayed believing that she had had her fair share of child raising.

Unquestionably, Cumquat—which she remained—was an unusual looking cat: she grew large and round and the relative size of her large paws did not diminish. Her harlequin-like face, orange on the right side, black on the left, combined with a somewhat patchy tortoiseshell body, meant that she could never be called beautiful, not even by Margot who adored her. As Cumquat grew older, a friend described her as the sort of woman who would slop around in slippers all day, cheeks rouged, lipstick alarmingly misdirected, with one false eyelash awry and a fag ever on the lip. Blossom Richardson fussed over her as a mother would over a plain daughter who never

left home. But in time, Cumquat looked the mother, and never-aging Blossom the kitten.

Added to this, Cumquat always had a wild look in her eyes as though she was about to attack you. But she had the gentlest nature and enjoyed being nursed, which meant that you often had to nurse both cats together and they made quite a bundle. She was an extremely companionable cat and liked to join in activities. If I were in the garden, she'd be investigating plants and bushes close by; whenever I was painting around the house she would climb the ladder and sit on the step just below me. She loved music and would lean against the piano when it was being played and sit on my feet when I played the violin. But she most enjoyed my singing, which possibly put her musical judgement in question. Whenever I burst forth in my robust baritone she would run to me, miaow to be picked up, and squirm until she was sitting on my cupped hands, squarely against my chest, forepaws pressed against my shoulders, her face only centimetres from mine, ears back, wild eyed, while the sound waves rolled around her.

Neither Blossom nor Cumquat were hunters. Only occasionally did one of them catch a mouse and rarely a bird. More than once I saw them sitting side by side on the lawn at night looking with mild interest at a bandicoot, a native marsupial that is commonly mistaken for a large rat, as it snuffled around looking for snails and burrowing for beetle larvae and insects with its long snout.

Dora didn't slip out of our lives entirely. She adapted readily to living on the Dennises' doorstep, or rather the landing with stone steps leading to the water under the converted boatshed.

I was unable to determine if she were pining for Charlie. She spent a lot of time foraging along the foreshore in company with the seagulls and somehow she did seem more relaxed, not as twitchy. I had thought that it would be a great relief for her to be rid of Charlie's excessive sexual demands but it's not easy to put yourself in a female duck's shoes, so to speak. There are women who will take an awful lot from their man, and occasionally I wondered if I had done the right thing in separating them. I felt particularly bad about Charlie's disappearance.

Something along these lines was going through my head one Saturday afternoon when, in a rare moment, I was lying on the terrace below the house, doing nothing, just looking up at the sky. A large flock of sulphur-crested cockatoos was wheeling raucously above the bay, their underwings flashing yellow as they dipped and soared and spontaneously changed direction again and again. I got to thinking how remarkable this was, this ability for dozens, hundreds, of birds to be flying along on, say, a nor'nor'west course then, in the flick of an eye, do a sudden about turn and wing off sou'sou'east.

The degree of concentration for a group of literal birdbrains was truly incredible, each and every one on their toes for whatever manoeuvre Leader Alpha Bravo out there in front was going to make next. I just couldn't see myself up there with them, putting my lack of feathers and total inability to fly to one side. I knew that I'd be cruising along nor'nor'west and my mind would drift off thinking how great it was to be flapping along look-no-hands a hundred metres up on a sunny summer's day, or speculating on the joys of raiding Farmer Brown's crop of maize come dusk when Leader Alpha Bravo would chuck a lefty and there I'd be in the middle of the flock still flapping dopily nor'nor'west. It would be total disaster.

I was more or less only half in focus as I pondered on this when precisely that happened. The entire flock bar one suddenly changed course and a lone bird continued to forge straight ahead, fortunately at a lower level than the rest. I blinked. It wasn't a cockatoo; it was Dora.

Aware that she was now on her own she wheeled around in what was for a her a tight turn and flapped furiously in the direction of the cockatoos who were by now on the far side of the bay. She had just caught up with them, but still at a lower altitude, when Leader Alpha Bravo took another tack and she again was left hurtling ahead.

Transparently, Dora had a need for company, but she had a major problem. Hans Christian Andersen's ugly duckling had the edge on her in that, even though it was a swan and not a duck, it was dead easy for it to join the duck club. But there was no way Dora was ever going to make it as a sulphur-crested cockatoo. This was made doubly clear when the flock above the bay suddenly screeched down to tree level and a dozen and one birds all but disappeared among the branches of the giant Moreton Bay fig. Had Dora followed she doubtless would have impaled herself or at least dislocated her hip joints. A cockatoo has four toes on each foot, two turning each way, designed to grab a branch and hang upside down if need be. Dora's big flat feet were designed to land on water, not solid wood.

I have developed a special affection for members of the parrot family, in particular *Cacatua galerita*, sulphur-crested cockatoos. They are the larrikins of Australia's skies, noisy, mischievous, gregarious, amusing, at times destructive without malice and with a will of their own.

The cocky is one of the most popular bird pets worldwide, and as the species live to the great age of eighty or even a hundred years, they very much become part of a family.

A friend of mine of mature years inherited the family cocky which had been sitting on its perch on the back verandah when he was born and was by now all but featherless. When my friend sold his house and moved into an apartment building where pets were not permitted he boarded Polly out but would visit her at weekends. Now, this man had considerable intellect and was a fierce debater with a fine command of language, but he would happily sit in front of the cocky cage by the half-hour exchanging the following brisk repartee:

COCKY: Put the kettle on, mate, put it on.
FRIEND: Does Polly want a cup of tea?
COCKY: A cuppa tea, a cuppa tea.
FRIEND: Does Polly want a scratch?
COCKY: Scratch cocky, scratch cocky.
And so on.

Stories of the extensive vocabularies of sulphur-crested cockatoos are legion and the birds have the flair to home in on phrases and sentences that are particularly apt. A West Australian friend of mine knew a cockatoo that lived in a pub in the goldmining town of Kalgoorlie. The bird was so old that it had scarcely a feather apart from its yellow crest, but it was still remarkably agile. When excited, it would parade up and down the bar flapping its little bare wings announcing, 'One day I'll fly. By god, one day I'll fly'.

On several occasions in the weeks ahead Dora would take off and endeavour to join the flock when the cockatoos came screeching into the bay. They never attempted to attack her the way birds commonly do when another species intrudes on their territory or feeding ground. I don't know if this is a characteristic of cockatoos because of their wide-ranging eating patterns: they themselves must repeatedly impinge on territory. On the practical side, they probably didn't see Dora as a threat. No way was she going to hang upside down from a branch nibbling figs.

Nature, it seems, abhors a duck vacuum, even a partial one. I was looking out at the harbour early one morning before leaving for the office when Dora appeared from around a headland which blocks the view into an adjoining bay. She was followed by another duck. I picked up the binoculars and focused. By now less of an innocent about such matters, I judged the second duck to be a male mallard. The mallard is a wild duck. I had an immediate reaction, and my innocence returned. Did ducks interbreed? Could a wild duck. . .?

Some weeks later the phone rang and the voice of Dora's foster-minder said: 'Would you care to come and see something?'

Lorna parted the honeysuckle which grew on the bank at the side of the Dennises' cottage. It was a familiar sight, a waterfall of white down and that glazed look of motherhood.

18

The great pork chop mystery

Margot was staring strangely at the two plates on the low occasional table in the living room where she had put them down in order to nick back into the kitchen for whatever it was she'd forgotten, which I gathered were the two dinner napkins she now had in her hand.

I could see her from the other side of the double glass doors where I was seated at the dining table salivating slightly in anticipation of a delicious dinner I had watched being prepared.

She shook her head as if to clear it, put the dinner napkins on the occasional table and went back into the kitchen. I could hear the griller door in the stove being opened and closed, then the door of the refrigerator, then various other doors.

She returned to the living room and again stared with what I interpreted as disbelief at the plates before making an odd sort of gurgling sound.

'What's wrong?' I called.

'One of them's gone,' she said.

'One what?'

'Pork chop. One has simply gone.'

'What do you mean gone?'

'Just that. It's disappeared. The pork chop has gone from your plate.'

'A likely story. Why my plate?'

'It was your plate because it had more on it.'

'Had?'

'Yes, had. That's the way it is.'

I pushed back my chair and went into the living room. On one of the plates, creamed potatoes topped by a whisk of parsley, a little sprig of broccoli, julienne carrots and a dob of apple sauce were tastefully arranged around a golden pork chop rimmed with crisp crackling.

On the other, a somewhat larger mound of creamed potatoes topped by a whisk of parsley, two sprigs of broccoli, marginally more julienne carrots and a considerable dob of apple sauce were tastefully arranged around—a space.

'That's mine?'

She nodded. 'Yes, that's yours.'

'Putting the question of equity on one side for the moment, er, how come?'

'It's a mystery. I dished up both plates, put them down for a moment to get the dinner napkins, and. . .it's gone.'

'You couldn't have served it. It must still be under the griller.' I was used to this sort of thing. My mother did it all the time. We'd have just finished the Sunday roast when mother would suddenly clutch her brow and declaim: '*Beans!*' We all knew what it meant. The beans were somewhere at the back of the wood-fueled stove, by now a green, gluggy mess glued to the bottom of a blackening saucepan.

I was heading for the kitchen when Margot said commandingly, 'Look!' and reaching down wiped her forefinger across the space on the plate. She held up the finger. 'Gravy! I tell you I served it.'

So someone was playing games. I went to the door, looked out, walked to the side of the house, looked up and down the path expecting to see one or other of my quainter friends sitting on a step munching a pork chop with relish. No one was to be seen.

The mystery of the missing pork chop remained unsolved.

✳ ✳ ✳

By now, after nearly three years in an office, I was once more working at home while Margot went into the city every day. I'd never felt at ease in my pinstripe suit in the executive suite. I'm just not a company man. Besides, I had plans for other projects.

Capping this, were the increasing difficulties of what had been a corporate marriage. Ours was not an uncommon chain of events: two people work closely together within an organisation, each respects the other's qualities and abilities, that respect develops into friendship, the inevitable drink after work to discuss an unresolved problem, then a bite of dinner the following week. . .

And next thing, there you are.

And there I was, not quite sure how I got there.

The respect and friendship remained, but increasingly we were each doing our own thing. We were two people floundering in different directions.

Floundering's hard.

It was perhaps a month after the pork chop incident. I had been working diligently all morning and when I stopped for lunch I had a sharper than usual appetite. Exploring the pantry shelves in the canned goods area I came across a small tin of pressed meats in aspic. Just the thing. I made up a salad comprised of a cupped lettuce leaf filled with grated carrot, some sliced tomato with fresh basil, several pieces of beetroot, and a hunk of cheese alongside a couple of pickled onions, tastefully arranged around the chubby, round portion of pressed meat.

I was rather pleased with all this and had left the kitchen heading for the dining room at the front of the house over-looking the harbour when I remembered the bread and the butter. I put the plate down on the low occasional table and went back into the kitchen.

As I emerged from the kitchen with the bread and butter I saw a long tongue shoot out, curl neatly around the chubby, round portion of pressed meat, and withdraw. It was like

watching a re-run of a film I had seen of a South American anteater demolishing a colony of ants.

'*Rummy!*' I roared.

He gulped—I could trace the path of the chubby, round portion of pressed meat down his gullet—and ran.

I was left staring down at the plate with the empty space surrounded by a cupped lettuce leaf filled with grated carrot, some sliced tomato with fresh basil, several pieces of beetroot, and a hunk of cheese alongside a couple of pickled onions.

Missing pork chop mystery resolved.

'I'll throttle you!' I shouted through the open door. Not a leaf stirred in the bushes growing thickly on the hillside. I went out into the courtyard, grabbed the garden hose, turned it on full and sprayed at random. There was a rustle and Rummy shot out of the bushes and up the path. 'Hah!' I shouted after him with some satisfaction. There was nothing he loathed more than a bath.

What was intriguing was how Rummy could enter the house and, in the case of the great pork chop mystery, neatly remove the chop and disappear within a matter of seconds without being seen or heard. I was well aware by now just how quietly a dingo moves. It wasn't simply the contrast between the way an affable little dog such as Archie the Australian terrier from next door would come bounding into the house all wags and wriggles and the way, say, the weimarana of another neighbour might walk in quietly, without fuss. Repeatedly, I would neither see nor hear Rummy come into the house or leave, and he was a frequent visitor. It wasn't as though he was sneaky; he simply had the capacity to glide in and out without his non-retractable claws tapping or scratching, without the sound of breathing, without creating a sense of movement. This is a characteristic for which dingoes are renowned in the wild.

As hunters, they exhibit remarkable patience and cunning. Depending on circumstances, a dingo might adopt totally different tactics. Rather than stalk a young calf which is keeping close to its mother, it might permit the cow to see it lying in the grass, sitting up having a scratch, walking around a little then flopping down again to rest, as if indifferent to her and her offspring. At first the cow will be wary and will continue to face the dingo, but as hours pass she will become accustomed to its presence and, as it doesn't seem to represent a threat, will relax her guard and start grazing. It is then the dingo strikes.

Now, was Rummy applying his inherent hunting skills to the domestic scene? Were my lunches and dinners under constant surveillance from somewhere out there in the bushes, or was it sheer chance that he just happened to drop by on those two occasions and, finding a tasty morsel at a convenient height on the low occasional table, was unable to resist the temptation? The incidents would never have occurred, of course, had he still been wearing his muzzle. Jock had given up on that. Rummy was older now, and had mellowed; also, his enemy, the red kelpie, had left the district. For Rummy's sake I thought it best not to mention the incidents to Jock.

Although Rummy was a great roamer, whenever Jock was at home the dingo would never be far from him. Their relationship, however, was not that of master–servant. In earlier years, I thought of Jock as Rummy's master and continued to refer to myself jokingly as deputy master. But no one ever really 'owns' a dingo. I was to learn that all successful relationships between the Australian native dog and man were more partnerships. I think both Jock and I regarded Rummy, not as a dog, but as our mate.

Rummy's domestication was not unique, but the degree to which he adapted to life in suburbia was certainly rare.

Even those who have a special affection for dingoes, such as Berenice Walters, of Bargo, New South Wales, who formed the Australian Native Dog Training Society in an endeavour to change the status of the animal, concedes that it is not a breed for the average pet owner.

Members of the society want the dingo removed from government 'vermin' and 'noxious' lists. They want an end to the trapping and mass aerial baiting. Largely, they want the dingo left alone, protected like other Australian native fauna, but they accept the need for culling should a renegade dog or pack prove to be a problem in a grazing area.

In recent years, scientific research has shown that stock comprises a very small proportion of the dingo's diet, that the animal much prefers native game. It is generally accepted that past figures of stock losses have been exaggerated, and some maintain that station dogs gone wild and crossbreeds are the dogs principally responsible for attacks on sheep and cattle.

Public opinion on dingoes was already changing when in August 1980, newspapers banner-headlined DINGO TAKES BABY and the case for acceptance of the animal simply as another breed of dog was put back decades.

The full sequence of events surrounding nine-week-old Azaria Chamberlain's disappearance from her carry basket in a tent on the outskirts of the camping ground at Ayers Rock in central Australia probably will never be known.

Early in the evening, Seventh Day Adventist pastor Michael Chamberlain and his wife Lindy were chatting with other campers when she left the group to check on Azaria who was asleep in the tent with her elder brother, Regan. Seconds later, the group heard Lindy cry, 'The dingo's got my baby!'

Two wild dogs had been seen near the camping ground that day. There was an immediate rush towards the low, vegetated sandhills just behind the camping ground in a bid to rescue Azaria.

The baby was never found.

The incident attracted enormous public attention and became highly controversial. Few accepted that a not-particularly-large dog could lift a baby neatly from a carry basket and disappear without trace. This was supported by a widely held belief that dingoes never attack humans.

But a coroner's inquest found that a dingo had taken Azaria.

A year later, the finding was reversed at a second inquest and Lindy Chamberlain was committed to trial for murder with her husband named as an accessory. In October 1982, the Chamberlains were found guilty as charged.

Nearly six years were to pass before the discovery of further evidence led to a Royal Commission which found that there was considerable support for the view that a dingo did take Azaria, and the convictions were quashed.

Roland Breckwoldt, who has studied the dingo intensively, and has a very balanced view on the animal's virtues and (in human terms) vices, was one of those who gave expert evidence for and against the dingo as the culprit.

Initially sceptical of the first coronial finding, Breckwoldt's subsequent studies of dingoes both in the wild and in a large enclosure on his property on the South Coast of New South Wales close to natural conditions, convinced him that dingoes could carry heavy objects with ease and commonly killed their prey without shedding blood.

Breckwoldt's experience with semi-wild dingoes that have become reliant on handouts of food led him to believe that it was credible that a dingo did take the Chamberlain baby from the tent. Even though the dingoes in his compound were well fed they were always alert for anything that smelled or looked like food. While never personally concerned by the possibility of attack, he says he would never risk leaving a small child alone with them, much less a baby.

My own *inexpert* view is that while I have known dingoes that, like Rummy, can be considered to be completely tame in their relationship with humans, one should remain a little wary of dingoes still living in the wild and dependent on hunting or scavanging for much of their food.

Unquestionably, the hunting instinct is strong in many breeds of dog—and man has cultivated it for his own ends. I've had two dogs, one a fox terrier and the other an unlikely pomeranian, that were demons among the neighbourhood poultry.

While accepting its hunting skills, unquestionably there are occasions when the dingo is not simply killing for food to survive, but attacking stock for the sheer hell of it. And these are the incidents that the grazier gripes about.

Invariably, there is a pair or a pack that will create havoc in a mob of sheep, ripping and tearing at one animal after another, leaving them to suffer appallingly slow deaths if they are not discovered by the landowner.

A cat will use a mouse as a plaything until it dies; killer whales behave in almost precisely the same way with baby seals. But the frenzied way dingoes will at times attack stock is different again. Abhorrent, yes, but think of the cruelty man is capable of inflicting, both on other creatures and his own kind.

When domesticated, the dingo is capable of great loyalty, but it remains very much its own person, an intelligent creature whose natural hunting and survival instincts have been finely honed. It is unreasonable to expect it to accept discipline in the same way as dogs that have been bred by man over many years for specific purposes.

Rummy seems to have been typical of his breed in that he was naturally well behaved in human terms. He never made a fuss: he fitted in. Ask him to do something and if it seemed reasonable he would comply. If it didn't seem reasonable, there was no way he could be made to do it.

With the dingo, the 'call of the wild' is always there, which was one of the reasons Jock was reluctant to take Rummy bush. It wasn't simply fear that someone would recognise him for what he was and take the law into their own hands. Jock was rightly concerned that if Rummy heard dingo howls while they were camping in the scrub that he could quietly, if reluctantly, slip away and never return.

This has been the experience of many a bushman who has acquired a dingo pup that has grown to become a much-loved companion.

The distinctive, drawn-out howl leaps into the mind as soon as the word 'dingo' is mentioned. Anyone who has heard the dogs in an isolated spot at night never forgets it. Dingoes are an extremely vocal breed. Domesticated dogs customarily howl when they are unhappy, usually when left alone, but dingoes howl to communicate.

Those who have studied dingoes say they actually have a wide range of howls. Apart from calling to each other to establish whereabouts for the purpose of hunting or mating, they often appear to howl for the pure joy of it. Calls have been described variously as singing, talking, yodelling, crowing.

Dingoes can bark, but seldom do. When they bark it comes out either as a single gruff woof or a high-pitched yap. They don't have the capacity to bark repetitively, and for this reason are not considered to be good watchdogs.

I heard Rummy bark on only a few occasions, and each time it was prompted by the barking of his labrador friend Blackie. Wanting to join in the fun, Rummy would give a single strained woof then immediately look embarrassed.

Oddly enough, contented dingoes sometimes purr. The gentle sound is different from a cat purr and appears to be made by the tongue vibrating against the teeth causing the lips to quiver.

There are other cat-like characteristics—their tactility, their ability to climb and spring, and the habit (I don't know if it is universal) of burying their faeces.

Rummy used his paws almost like hands. When he wanted to attract your attention he would tap you on the knee or, if you were seated, place a paw on your thigh; he would tap at a door to let you know he was there. He could turn doorknobs and open gate latches. Strange things were investigated with

a paw, and perhaps the non-retractable claws made it relatively easy for him to pick things up.

Not having another dingo with whom to communicate Rummy seldom howled but when he did his breed was unmistakable.

One afternoon Jock and I went fishing at a deep hole well out in the harbour. Rummy didn't like water. It wasn't simply that he didn't like swimming or being bathed; he seemed to regard water as an unnatural element. It distressed him when any member of the family was in a boat.

This particular afternoon he was beside himself when two of his best mates took to sea. He ran along the shoreline as we moved up the harbour, scrambling over rocks, pounding over sandy stretches, thrashing through bushes where they crowded the shore. Eventually, he found a jetty that was the closest point to us and sat on the end with his head tilted back and howled and howled and howled.

Rummy had never known life in the wild, but he certainly knew how dingoes communicate.

19

At the bottom of the garden. . .

A pixie suddenly appeared beside me, which in a way should not have been surprising because I was at the bottom of the garden. 'May I help you?' he said politely in a small but confident voice. This was a relief, because he obviously was a good fairy, that is, pixie. He had a little white face with sharp features and serious dark-brown eyes, and was wearing an outsize football guernsy, football socks and boots, and a beanie with a pompom on top going straight up like a witch's hat.

'Thank you,' I said, equally politely. 'You could help me rake up the leaves for burning if you wish.'

'A lot do fall down,' he said matter-of-factly, and without further ado picked up a rake and went to work.

I was speculating which toadstool he lived under when he volunteered without a pause in the raking, 'My name is Marcus. I'm seven and three quarters. I live over there now.' He tilted his beanie towards a house on the waterfront further into the bay between Bruce Pearce's land and Richardson's. A family had moved in some weeks before but I hadn't met them; in fact, I had never met their predecessors. I recalled that someone had told me the newcomer was a doctor.

We exchanged small talk as we worked, me pulling weeds out of a patch of earth I whimsically called a garden, he raking up the leaves that fell endlessly from the trees. Yes, he liked living in the bay. Yes, he liked swimming but preferred fishing. No, he wasn't playing football yet; besides it wasn't the football season. The football gear he was wearing belonged to his next older brother James. He told me there were five boys and a girl in the family, and they had a dog and a cat, but I concluded after further conversation that one of the 'boys' was the father and the 'girl' was the mother.

All the time he raked away industriously, at intervals carrying a bundle of leaves to a pile for burning. Then he said, 'My biggest brother Simon says that when he grows up he is either going to be a policeman or God.'

'That's ambitious,' I said, impresed.

He paused in the raking. 'What's ambitious?'

'Let's say, being ambitious is wanting to do something important or to be someone important.' He nodded gravely, accepting this. 'But why does he want to be either a policeman or God?'

'My brother Simon says that people have only got two bosses—policemen and God.' He nodded again, indicating that he had thought the matter through. 'I think he will be a policeman.'

'And what are you going to be?' I asked, 'A doctor like your father?'

He considered this for a moment or two, leaning on the rake, then said, 'No. I think I'll be something with a siren and a flashing light on top.' Then he continued raking up the leaves.

In response to my knock, the door was opened by a handsome woman with well-groomed fair hair. She was wearing an apron and holding a wooden spoon vertically like a baton in a relay race. Only she was licking it.

'Oh!' she said. 'Caught out! I thought it was one of the boys. I'd locked the door to keep them at bay. When *I* choose to lick the spoon it drives the three of them mad.'

'Looks delicious,' I said. 'What's it to be?'

'Marble cake.'

'Umm! One of my favourites. How fortunate I'm living almost next door.' She inclined her head with humour in her eyes, and opened the door wide. 'I've met Marcus, so I thought I should call and say hello, and welcome to the bay.' And I introduced myself.

'I'm Fiona Fisher.' A bright smile; her voice had a soft hint of a Scottish accent. 'Do come in; the cake will be out of the oven shortly.'

The non-spoon-licking Marcus was sitting on a high stool at a bench on the far side of the kitchen, where I guessed the family ate breakfast and snacks, reading a very large book. Facing me, he looked up with his dark, intelligent eyes, smiled by way of recognition, and resumed reading his book.

Fiona indicated a high stool opposite Marcus. 'Do you mind if I finish tidying up? Then I'll put on the kettle.'

From my perch I looked down at the book Marcus was reading. It was *The Complete Works of William Shakespeare*. 'This is impressive,' I said.

'He's decided to be an actor,' said Fiona. She glanced at the book. 'Marcus believes in starting at the top, don't you dear?'

Marcus nodded and continued reading.

'Yesterday,' I said, 'he told me he wanted to be something with a siren and a flashing light on top.'

'That was yesterday,' said Fiona. 'Today, he rather fancies being Henry the Fifth.'

As she washed several bowls I told her what a great help Marcus had been the previous day raking the fallen leaves.

'Really?' she said, turning to look at her son with raised eyebrows. 'I didn't realise he knew what raking was. Certainly, none of his brothers do.'

'Well, I can only say he's a fine lad, a great little worker.'

She cocked her head to one side. 'Indeed?. . .Umm, he's actually the butter-wouldn't-melt-in-your-mouth type. Excuse me a moment.'

Marcus just kept on reading.

Fiona left the kitchen and walked down the hall. She returned carrying a small cardboard box which she opened then dropped its contents on the workbench between Marcus and me. It was a funnel-web.

I jumped back from the stool, whipped off one of the rubber thongs I was wearing, and slapped it down on the spider. It felt sort of funny. I pulled the thong away. The spider was unsquashed. I looked at her, still startled, puzzled.

'Oh, I am sorry,' she said. 'I thought you'd recognise it immediately. What an appalling way to treat a welcoming neighbour! But, in effect, that is what my little darlings have been doing to me since we arrived here.' She pointed a finger at Marcus, who was grinning broadly. '*He's* the worst offender.' I was looking at the object on the bench; it was an an amazingly accurate rubber replica of a funnel-web, the sort of thing you can buy in a so-called fun store. 'You'd think I'd be used to it by now. Once a week, it seems, when I'm getting into bed I pull back the bedclothes and there it is. I scream *every* time. Clearly I have no self-control.'

'Why don't you simply take it from them and put it in the garbage bin?' I said.

She thought for a moment. 'Umm, but that would be the easy way out, wouldn't it? I think I'm deluding myself that I've turned it into an exercise in resisting temptation. But they're disgustingly weak. I fine them five cents of their pocket money—all four of them—for each offence, but they seem to think my reactions are worth it. I wish I had your presence of mind and could slap it with a slipper. . .Tea?'

We sat on the verandah eating marble cake that marginally had been given time to cool and sipping tea of an unusual but extremely pleasant flavour. She blended her own, she said, using a little of this and a little of that. And we talked about the charm of the bay and the wildlife, about which she had more-than-average knowledge. Dora came swimming along the foreshore with several of her half-grown progeny clearly sired by the mallard drake. 'I've heard the ducks are yours,' she said.

'Not at all,' I protested, 'although I guess I have a degree of responsibility.' And I told her briefly of Dora's arrival and subsequent history.

'We should talk more,' she said. 'We want to learn about the area. Would you care to come to dinner, just something simple, say, tomorrow night and meet Garrath?' Her lips quivered a little at the corners, and it was clear where her boys' sense of michief came from. 'It should be a mild night, so with luck we will have a spider supper on the verandah.'

Glancing at the rubber funnel-web still on the kitchen bench, I took this to be a slip of the tongue. Surely she meant to say 'won't' not 'will'.

Four more well-mannered boys you could not wish to meet, all tall like their father who had the lean physique of an athlete; a serious man, but with a quick, ready smile. The boys shook hands and said good evening, chatted intelligently for some ten minutes, then went off to do their homework, the younger two being instructed not to forget to have their bath before going to bed.

I sorted out their names in descending order as Garrath poured a pre-dinner drink—Simon the eldest, he who was intent on being a policeman or God, then Tom, James and Marcus. I commented that Tom had a bit of the devil in his eye.

'Hmmm, Tom,' said Fiona. 'As a toddler he seemed convinced that he could fly. He kept launching himself from his cot. We finally put his mattress on the floor.'

Fiona led the way on to the verandah where a table was beautifully set. 'As the guest, you must have the box seat,' indicating a chair. 'Garrath thinks it's rather like being in the Roman coliseum but I don't think it really can be compared with throwing Christians to the lions.' And a hand waved towards the steel railing surrounding the verandah, or rather the space above it. A magnificent spider web filled the space between the rail and the overhanging gutter, with a large orb-weaver at home in the centre.

'What a perfect web,' I said.

'I thought you'd appreciate it,' said Fiona. 'It's been there for some days and we dine together in the evenings. We've, well, sort of become friends. Or rather we're like people who regularly have adjoining tables in a restaurant but never get around to meeting.'

Garrath laughed. 'I don't know about dining in a restaurant. Seems to me that with Robert the Bruce over there it's more like Dial-a-Pizza.'

Just then a moth flew into the web no doubt attracted by the light on the verandah. 'Ah, the first course,' said Garrath. The spider ran lightly across the web. The attack was swift; the struggle brief. Immediately, the spider began spinning a silken cocoon around the moth.

'Not the first course,' I said. 'It's clearly keeping it for afters.'

Over dinner we soon left the subject of spiders to discuss other local wildlife. Like Fiona, Garrath had a good general knowledge of both Australian fauna and flora; they were clearly delighted with their move to the bay. We talked about its history, broadly who the neighbours were—although they had no interest in gossip—and got around to sailing which they were very keen to do. Yes, they would love to come out on my ketch. It was clear we were to be friends.

As Fiona was serving coffee, the murmur of boys' voices came from inside the house and the sound of running water filling a bath. The voices rose until there were sharp, shrill exchanges.

'Trouble at mill,' Fiona observed.

'Excuse me,' Garrath said to me, and called, 'Quiet boys!' Adding, 'This is unusual; they're the best of friends.'

Then Marcus screamed, 'I'll kill you! I'll get the gun! I'll kill you!'

And I thought, Is this really the little pixie from the bottom of the garden?

'Quiet!' shouted Garrath. Then the sound of running down the hall. 'Whatever are they up to?'

'I guess Marcus has gone to get the gun,' Fiona said matter-of-factly.

'The what?' said Garrath.

'The gun. He was playing with it this afternoon. His friend

Rupert lent it to him. Amazing the toys they're making. It looks like the real thing.'

'They should be banned,' Garrath rumbled.

Running feet back along the hall. Then a screamed 'I told you I would!' And the explosive sound of a gun fired in a confined space, the smell of cordite, and another, ghastly, scream.

'Oh my god!' said Fiona, and our chairs went flying as the three of us rushed into the house.

Marcus was leaning against the doorway opening into the bathroom. His face was very white. He was gripping a snub-nosed revolver with his two small hands; the tip of a finger was on the trigger. He looked up and said, 'I warned him! I told him I would!'

James was slumped in the bath, eyes closed. A crimson mass oozed down his chest.

Fiona was on her knees beside the bath, cradling James. 'Garrath! Do something!' she shouted at her doctor husband.

Garrath took the pistol from Marcus's hands, glanced at it, then leaned over the bath. His fingers opened one of the boy's closed eyes which fell shut as he released it. He looked closely at the crimson chest then turned and walked out of the bathroom.

'Garrath!' Fiona called frantically.

He was back in seconds, gripping a leather belt. Leaning over Fiona, her dress now drenched, crimson stained, he drew a finger across James's chest and held it under her nose.

She sniffed, then exclaimed, '*Tomato sauce!* You little beasts!'

Garrath took the murder weapon from his pocket and showed it to Fiona. 'It's a starter's pistol,' he said. 'It fires blanks.'

Marcus the actor was again racing down the hall, now pursued by his father who, I could swear, had a siren—and a flashing light on top.

20

A possum dosshouse

'Are you really sleeping in here?' I asked incredulously.

'Certainly,' said Jock.

Plop went a drop in a bucket.

'It strikes me as being a variant of Chinese water torture.'

'Indeed?' said Jock. 'That hadn't occurred to me.'

Above us, winter rain was beating rhythmically on the galvanised iron roof. I could visualise the puddles in the cane-fibre ceiling which were causing it to sag giving the impression that stalactites were forming where the water was seeping through.

Pling went a drop in another bucket.

'I can see that it represents a challenge.'

'Well,' said Jock with some pride, 'the floor is bone dry.'

Plong went a drop in yet another bucket.

'That says a lot for your keen eye. But then you were a bomber pilot.'

'Tonight,' Jean said emphatically, '*I* am sleeping in the next room.'

I counted the puddles in the ceiling. There were seven, directly above buckets placed around the room like chessmen on a king-sized concrete chessboard in a public park.

'Well,' I said. 'I agree that the place needs a new roof.'

Jock shrugged and lit a cigarette.

Jean glanced at him. 'We really wonder if it's worth it,

which is why we kept putting off doing it. We never thought of *you* buying the house. Jock thought the new owner would simply knock it down. It's so old and there's so much wrong with it.'

'That's what I've been telling him for months,' Jock grumbled, 'but I haven't even been able to get him to *look* at the place.'

This was quite true: inspection had seemed superfluous as I thought I knew the house so well. I had decided to buy the property when Jock and Jean told me they were subdividing into three blocks and building a new house at road level. Jock had taken early retirement; the countless number of cigarettes he had chain-smoked throughout a lifetime had done nothing to improve his health. But I saw what I was purchasing as simply a block of land; there was no point in inspecting the house. At least I think that was what I thought. Numbed by the situation with Margo, of late I hadn't been quite sure what I was thinking.

I looked around the room at the dripping ceiling, the buckets, filled with niggling doubts, then followed Jock on the long-deferred tour of inspection.

Are you sure you're doing the right thing I asked myself. Then I rationalised that I had been in the bay for eight years by now, I loved the area, and it was only commonsense to have a stake in the place.

But it did seem to be one heck of a time to be buying a house. Margot had moved into an apartment; I was again on my own. Was I going to rattle around in this old barn with a pair of cats for company?

Margot will want Cumquat, I told myself, but I knew that she couldn't bear to separate her from Blossom. They were like Siamese twins.

Only half-listening to Jock, I seemed to be hearing the real-estate chestnut of a house being a renovator's dream— meaning nightmare.

Maybe I could do just a few essential things I thought, justifying my course of action, live in it for a while, then build a new place some time in the future when life had sorted itself out.

Jock was pointing at the splendidly flamboyant patterns on the pressed metal walls and ceiling which were a feature of the living room, and reminding me that the house had been built early in the century by a stage manager of J. C. Williamson's, once Australia's foremost firm of theatrical entrepreneurs. The large central living room, nearly ten metres long and more than six metres wide with a four-metre-high ceiling, was the heart of the house which was clearly designed for entertaining. The one-time stage where Nellie Melba had sung was now the dining area adjoining the kitchen that Jock had added. Previously, like many colonial houses, the wood-burning stove had been on the back verandah to minimise the risk of fire.

We moved into the kitchen. A possum tail was dangling through the hole in the ceiling, a long-familiar sight. Jock didn't seem to notice it so I endeavoured not to look at it as we inspected the kitchen and agreed with him that it could do with a dramatic face lift.

I looked up at the tail. 'I hope you're taking Edgar with you.'

Nibbles had moved out—or on—some years before.

'He's not a problem,' said Jock.

'It's a matter of personal preference. I'd just as soon not have a possum tail suspended above the frying pan while I'm cooking *my* bacon and eggs.'

'He's in the *centre* of the ceiling, over the floor.'

I looked up at Edgar's tail. 'True.' Jock had already proved his eye for the vertical line with the buckets in the bedroom.

He drew on his cigarette. 'Perhaps I should mention Clippy.'

'Clippy?'

'I call her Clippy. She's no trouble at all, really. She likes the wall cavity beside the fireplace.' Jock jerked his head for me to follow and walked back into the living room.

The wide skirting board alongside the fireplace that backed on to the kitchen had been pushed out from the wall by a bulge of grey fur. A protruding black-tipped tail was draped across the floor. 'Clippy?' I said.

Jock nodded. 'She's a pretty little thing, but she's got one clipped ear. At least it looks clipped. It probably was torn in a fight, or perhaps when mating.'

'Are they the only two in residence?'

'That I know of.'

'Then as you see it Edgar and Miss Clippy go with the house.'

Jock thought for a moment. 'You could block them out if you really wanted to.'

'A point. I've bedded down in some funny places but so far I've avoided a possum dosshouse.'

Jock shrugged.

For the next hour or so I followed Jock from room to room, crawled around the ceiling, and wormed my way through the Aladdin's cave of treasures he just couldn't bear to throw away which were crammed under the house. And as the inspection progressed, an interesting role reversal developed with Jock, the seller, highlighting flaws while I, the buyer, found myself glossing over them with remarks such as, 'It's not so bad'. . .'Nonsense, I could soon fix that'. . .'A mere detail'. . .'There's nothing in replacing a ceiling'. . .'Sound as a bell'. . .'Needs a lick of paint'. . .'So it's made of timber. In Europe, I've seen wooden houses that have stood for centuries'. . .

True, there was a lot of work to be done because the Muirs had long neglected maintenance in anticipation of their move, but essentially the building was sound. Minute by minute, my earlier attitude changed and I found myself working the old place over in my mind: I revamped the kitchen and bathroom, converted the down-at-heel laundry to a second bathroom, switched the fourth bedroom to a snug sunroom, turned Jock's jam-packed work area into a dining room, and transformed the leaking main bedroom into an office with superb views over the harbour.

Honest Jock had overstated the decrepitness of the structure. By the time the tour had concluded I had found to my surprise, that I had bought myself, not just a block of land, but a charming old house.

An apple was lying alongside the fruit bowl on the dining table. Or rather half an apple with a set of tooth marks. It was clear who the culprit was. 'So!' I muttered. 'You're not content with free lodgings, you're into midnight snacks as well.'

The skirting board was pushed out from the wall alongside the fireplace even more than usual revealing a grey bulge of possum. I got my toolbox from the workbench under the house, pushed the skirting board with my foot against the pressure of an expanded midriff, and belted in a couple of nails. The possum stirred, but there was no frantic scramble to escape up the wall cavity. Miss Clippy, it seemed, was tolerant of the eccentric behaviour of human beings.

But not Edgar. As Nibbles' successor to the ceiling accommodation he had grown accustomed to five-star treatment and clearly expected established standards to be maintained. At dusk on my first day of occupancy in my new house a paw appeared through the hole in the ceiling and waved around, claws and pink pads contracting in a clutching movement. 'Room service,' I said, addressing the ceiling, 'has been discontinued. The establishment is under new management.'

The paw was retracted, then the other one was thrust through the hole and repeated the waving patterns. 'I think you should understand, Edgar,' I continued, 'that you're living on borrowed time. As soon as I can get around to it you're being evicted.' I then started preparing the evening meal hoping the paw would go away. After a minute or two it was withdrawn and I heard Edgar scrabbling along the ceiling cavity between the joists and performing the 180-degrees contortionist trick that enabled him to clamber on to the roof. Footsteps along the corrugated iron, then one of the oleander bushes that had grown to the size of trees along Bruce Pearce's boundary shook as the possum leapt the gap. A rustling of leaves. Then stomp, stomp, stomp. Edgar had come in through the open laundry door and was marching on all fours through to the living room.

I walked to the edge of the dining area that had once been a stage to meet him. The possum marched up to me, sat on its haunches and looked up at me inquiringly. It seemed surprised at seeing a stranger. 'If you want to complain to the manager,' I said, 'you're wasting your time. The Muirs' have moved to the new house up the hill. I suggest you stroll up and enquire about the catering arrangements. And see if they have a ceiling vacancy while you're about it.'

Edgar listened to this intently then got down on all fours and sniffed at my shoes and trouser legs before again sitting up and looking at me expectantly. 'No,' I said. 'Not a skerrick of lettuce *or* apple. I know what the thin edge of a wedge can do: I've been that way with ducks. Now I suggest you just carry on through and go about your nightly business.' And I walked to the open glass door that led on to the verandah with Edgar following. When he was outside I slipped back in, closed the door, and walked through to lock the laundry door as well. For the foreseeable future it was clear that, come sunset, I had to batten down all hatches.

The strategy worked. Simply by placing a lettuce leaf or two and the odd piece of fruit in the fork of the jacaranda tree that grew in front of the house I had been able to divert Edgar from first thumping on the laundry door then, when that failed to attract attention, pressing his pink nose against the glass to stare at me through the double verandah doors.

At dusk he now clambered on to the roof, stomped around to the front of the house, reached up a paw to one of the jacaranda branches overhanging the verandah and climbed across to his supper.

I had soon learned that the roof was regarded locally as the possum promenade.

The centre section was a hip roof that covered the large central room. It was encircled by a skillion or nearly flat roof like the brim of a hat covering the rest of the house. The skillion roof was the connecting path between all the surrounding trees—the jacaranda at the front, the two giant camphor laurels that grew to the left of it and the liquid amber on the next terrace down, the two poplar trees near the bedrooms, the tree-sized oleanders along the kitchen and bathroom side, and more camphor laurels, eucalypts and shrubs on what was still the Muirs' land at the back.

Rather than climbing to the ground and walking on the grass to the next tree beyond leaping distance or to a tree on the opposite side of the house, the possum population found it convenient to drop on to the roof and stroll across.

I became aware of all this on the first night in the house when, at intervals, I would snap awake at the sound of footsteps convinced that I was about to be carried off by marauding Mongols.

It must have been three in the morning when the Mongols suddenly charged full belt, galloping around the roof, then back again, then around once more. And then straight up the hip roof and down the other side and back again, up and over, the screeching of scratched metal like the scouring of a thousand saucepans setting my teeth on edge.

A moment's silence. Then the deep guttural coughs and sharp hisses of the amorous Edgar, I assumed, winning the heart of his lady love. Was it Miss Clippy?

21

The halfway station

'Hello,' I said to the total stranger walking through the living room.

He looked at me, surprised. 'Oh! Are you staying with Eric?'

'No. I'm staying with me. Eric doesn't live here. He's down on the waterfront.'

'You mean this isn't the waterfront?'

'You could call it the halfway station. But now you're inside you might as well carry on through. The path is in front. Just keep going.'

Eric Seymour, a bachelor, had bought the cottage on the third block below my house that had been created by the Muirs' subdivision. Neat ruled lines along the western boundary of the official plan represented a fictitious path leading from the road to the harbour foreshore.

In practice, Eric and I continued to use the path that had been in existence for the better part of a century. It led from the road down along the eastern side of the Muirs' new house to my back door. To reach his block, Eric walked on the lawn around my house and linked up with the path leading from my front steps to the waterfront.

This was totally confusing to Eric's visitors. Once they reached my house they couldn't see where else to go, and in any case they felt they had gone far enough. 'Not *more* steps!'

they would cry when told they were only halfway there, as though it was all my fault.

The local dogs felt the same way. It was understandable that Rummy would continue to wander through; he had been raised in the house and my relationship with his family was so close that when I moved in he probably assumed that Jock and Jean had finally legally adopted me. But all his pals had the same viewpoint, including the boxer owned by Fiona and Garrath Fisher. Why walk around, they apparently thought, when you can take a short cut? Time and again, some pooch or other that I'd scarcely met would just wander through, in one door and out the other, barely giving me a sideways glance.

They had the same attitude to the skillion roof. It was possum territory at night, but during the day the domestic animals regarded the eastern side, which was sheltered from most winds, as their sundeck. Only a moderate jump was required to reach the roof from the terrace at the back of the house. When Jock added his workroom to the original dwelling, he had taken it right to the terrace and incorporated the fine stone retaining wall in the structure. It became the back wall of the room which opened on to a courtyard shaded by a magnificent wisteria vine and was designated my future dining room.

Most of my grand renovation plans remained in the future. Knowing the way I invariably approach things I was determined not to commit myself to an exhausting work program trying to do too much in too short a time. I had the greater part of the galvanised-iron roof replaced, painted the large living room—a task which might be equated with Michelangelo's dabbling in the Sistine Chapel—put a new ceiling in what had been the main bedroom and converted the room into my office.

This was luxury, a spacious room in which I could leave my work undisturbed. I fitted bookshelves and all the office paraphernalia and built my desk against the wall across the front of the house and along one side under wide windows that looked out through the jacaranda and camphor laurels, a liquid amber and tall pines to the harbour beyond.

The months passed pleasantly as I grew to know and appreciate the charming old house with all its faults. Margot and I were having a degree of success in re-converting our marriage into a friendship and she was a frequent visitor. At weekends I sailed, or had friends to dinner, or lunched on the wide verandah, or barbecued on the terrace under the leafy liquid amber. Life was very agreeable.

It would be extreme to say I was camping in the house, but things remained pretty basic. After the first burst of activity which took care of essentials, the renovation program slowed to a halt. I felt no pressure to launch into phase two.

Things might have remained this way for much longer had it not been for Edgar. He still lodged in the kitchen ceiling and on occasions his tail would dangle through to the startlement of visitors, but he had given up demanding food.

One morning when work had ground to a halt and I was wondering if life might not be more fulfilling as a streetsweeper in Bombay or a deckhand on an Arab dhow, I drifted towards the kitchen with the vague intention of making a cup of coffee.

As I stepped on to the dining area a stream of amber liquid poured to the floor through the ragged hole in the kitchen ceiling.

'*Edgar!*' I roared. 'Where are your manners? Have you become incontinent in old age or is this your opinion of the catering arrangements? Enough! Out! Out!' And I grabbed the broom and thumped the ceiling until the startled Edgar scrambled out on to the roof. Then I got the stepladder and my tools and immediately began tearing the dilapidated kitchen apart. The Great Possum War had begun.

The renovations were an unqualified success: the kitchen was transformed. I put in new cupboards, scraped layers of paint off the Dutch dresser to reveal its mellow timber, installed a new sink and a dishwasher, laid floor tiles—and fitted a possum-proof ceiling.

Within a few days of packing up my tools I heard a soft scrabbling sound above me as I stepped under the shower. So! Edgar, Miss Clippy, or one of their kind, had moved into the adjoining apartment in the bathroom ceiling. I determined to take action before the new tenant gained the impression it had a permanent let.

Margot came for the weekend to admire and put the kitchen to the test. She brought a new friend. He was red-headed, handsome, intelligent, athletic and self-confident to the point of brashness. He was six weeks old.

She put Rufus on the floor of the living room just inside the door. Blossom and Cumquat were together, as always, at the far end of the room. They took one look at the kitten, drew up their skirts and hissed their disapproval. Rufus had seen them and had crouched the way lions crouch with body all aquiver when about to leap on their prey. Suddenly, he darted the length of the room, pounced on their twitching tails, wrestled their hindquarters and stood on his hind legs to bat their ears. They were not amused. It could be said it was hate at first sight. They knew all about *men*.

But Rufus was irrepressible. He plagued the two cats mercilessly, stopping only when he fell suddenly and deeply asleep the way kittens do. Awake again, he would resume his tormenting.

Cumquat gained some respite in the afternoon when she came outside to help me prepare the lengths of timber to block the entrances to the gaps between the bathroom roof and ceiling. She was a very companionable cat who enjoyed human activity. If I was sawing a piece of wood she would sit nearby and watch the saw going up and down; if I was painting a ceiling she would climb the stepladder and sit on the step just below me. Despite her bulk she was very adept at climbing stepladders.

My plan was to cut the timber to size, wait until the possum occupant or occupants had left for the evening, then nail the timber in place.

Margot and I were enjoying a gin and tonic on the verandah watching flying foxes crossing the harbour in the light of an early risen half-moon when we heard the familiar sound of footsteps overhead. There was a rustle in the jacaranda tree and we could see the silhouette of a possum as it made its way from branch to branch across to the adjacent camphor laurel. I waited for another half hour to give any other freeloader time to leave then went down, climbed the extension ladder that I had left in position, and nailed the pieces of timber over the gaps.

In the early hours of the morning I awakened to the soft thump of a possum jumping on to the roof from one of the camphor laurel trees. It padded around to the other side of the house and I could hear a scrabbling sound then a rushing around which became increasingly frantic. Finally, quiet. I had won.

I woke early as usual with a quiet sense of accomplishment. I was making acceptable progress on the house: the kitchen had been renovated, the place was now possum-proof. I left Margot sleeping, tiptoed past the kitten still asleep in its basket, and went out on to the verandah to enjoy the morning light and the superb chorus of kookaburras, magpies, currawongs, rainbow lorikeets and half a dozen other species of bird that marked the start of every day. Then I went to the bathroom noting with satisfaction that there were no sounds coming from the ceiling as I showered and began to shave, singing softly to myself so as not to disturb Margot.

My face was well lathered when I heard miaowing. I opened the door a little thinking one of the cats was saying good morning, but neither was there, so I closed it again.

The miaowing persisted, more loudly, as I continued shaving: it was coming from outside. I glanced to my left and saw Cumquat at the window. She had climbed the extension ladder which I had left against the wall and was miaowing at me through the glass louvres. 'How did you get up there you fat old thing?' I said.

At the sound of my voice she heaved herself further up the

ladder her paws slipping precariously on the narrow, round timber rungs.

'You'll fall off,' I said. 'It's not a *step*ladder.' Whereupon she launched herself through a gap between the rungs, her forepaws landing on one of the glass plates in the half-open window. A kick with her hind legs against a ladder rung and the louvres tilted open as she slid forward between two sheets of glass.

I dropped my razor and went to the window to pull her through. But she was too fat: she was wedged.

The only thing was for her to go out backwards but she had lost her footing on the ladder.

Jammed between the glass plates like the frankfurt in a hot dog she panicked. I tried to support her, but all four paws with claws extended were flailing like a swimmer who has incomprehensibly run out of water. I risked being torn to shreds. 'Steady down,' I ordered. 'If the glass breaks you'll end up a harakiried cat.'

She flailed even more wildly. This wasn't a one-man job. Arching my arm to stay clear of the claws I got a grip of the back of her neck and called calmly, 'Margot.' No response.

Louder. 'Margot!' Still no response. She was on the far side of the house with the bathroom door and the bedroom door between us, dead to the world.

Wild-eyed, Cumquat squirmed and flailed, fighting against my grip.

'*Margot!*' I bellowed. '*Can—you—help—me?*' They probably heard me across the bay.

There was a thud as her feet hit the floor.

'Easy on, Cumquat!' I said. 'Easy on! The cavalry's coming.'

And it might have been. The bedroom door was flung open as Margot came running. As always she was moving at the speed of light.

She ran across the living room.

She ran past the bathroom.

Eh?

She wrenched open the back door.

She ran up the steps to the terrace.

She scrambled on to the roof.

And she ran around the roof calling, 'Where are you?'. . . 'What's happened?'. . .'Where *are* you?'

'I'm down here,' I shouted. 'I'm in the bathroom!'

'Where?'

'The bathroom. I'm in the *bathroom*! What on earth are you doing up there?'

She was on her knees, I assume, peering over the edge. 'I thought you'd fallen off the roof. You haven't?'

'If I had I wouldn't be up there, would I?'

'Oh.' A pause. 'Silly. I was sound asleep. All I could think of when I heard you calling was the roof and you working up the ladder.'

Cumquat was fast getting out of control. 'Since you're up there would you please climb down it, the ladder. And on your way past grab the stern end of this cat of yours.'

We somehow threaded Cumquat back out through the louvres unharmed.

The soap had dried like parchment on my face. As I washed it off and began lathering up again to finish my shave I heard a snarl, a hiss, and scampering of little feet. Young Rufus had resumed harassment.

* * *

Leaning on the verandah railing eating grapes and spitting the pips with satisfying accuracy to land dead in the centre of a May bush I noticed Guy Irving paddling out into the harbour in his canoe.

It was something of a mystery just why a handsome, personable young man with a social background and the inheritor of a prosperous business had decided to buy the block of Squire Wilcox's now-subdivided property which was comprised of the two undistinguished houses I had lived in for eight years.

Even more surprising was the fact that he chose to live in the primitive little cottage on the waterfront and rent out the larger house further up the hill; with his dashing red sports car and well-cut suits he was far more luxury apartment.

The attraction of pip-spitting faded as I looked down at Guy in his canoe. It was the sort of canoe that I had coveted since boyhood, the type built by North American Indians from the bark of the birch tree and subsequently utilised by fur traders and Canadian mounties intent on getting their man.

Boyhood friends had owned such a canoe and I had regarded them with envy. Unfortunately, I mostly saw the beautiful canoe at a distance because when we went on expeditions to the upper reaches of Queensland's Brisbane River it was always far out in front.

While my young mate and I worked like galley slaves thrashing the water with crude homemade paddles to push our own cranky craft along, the Canadian canoe glided on the horizon.

Our canoe was made from a flattened sheet of discarded corrugated roofing iron, the nail holes plugged with bitumen dug from the roadway on a hot day.

Watching Guy as he passed my much-loved ketch riding at its mooring, I was admiring the canoe's smooth lines and the upsweep of the curved bow and stern when it occurred to me that it was riding extremely low in the water. I went inside for my binoculars. No wonder the canoe was riding low; it was loaded almost to the gunnels with oyster shells raked from the foreshore where Guy was making a shark-proof netted swimming pool. His intention obviously was to dump the shells in deep water. I sniffed trouble.

One of the great pastimes on the waterfront is watching how others go about things, often with a curl of the upper lip and a scornfully muttered, 'What the hell *does* he think he's doing?' The waterfront is an area where everyone. is an expert on everything.

I put down the binoculars and resumed grape eating and pip spitting, letting the pips fall where they may, while I considered the situation. It was clear that yet again Guy had not thought things through. Shovelling oyster shells into the canoe in shallow water presented little difficulty. Getting them out of the overladen, far-from-stable vessel was another matter.

Across the bay, I could see parallel lines moving in Guy's direction, the wash from a launch that had disappeared around the headland.

The wash reached Guy just as he came alongside a large mooring buoy. The canoe rocked wildly. Guy clutched at the buoy and endeavoured to scramble on to it presumably to lighten the load. As he transferred his weight the port gunnel went under, water poured aboard, and that beautiful Canadian canoe disappeared forever to settle on the bed of the harbour twenty metres below.

It would be wrong to say that Guy was accident prone. The mishaps that plagued him were not accidents, they were self-inflicted.

On a number of occasions I set out for my early morning walk to find Guy's snappy sports car parked askew to the footpath with the front bumper bar hard against the rear bumper bar of the car in front. There was no damage: it seemed that the sports car had simply come gently to rest being unable to proceed any further because of the obstruction. The roof was folded down, jacket and tie were on the back seat along with his briefcase, his wallet was lying invitingly on the front passenger seat.

The paths and steps didn't bother Guy nor, apparently, the procession of gorgeous girls who made their way down to the harbourside cottage. But all were clearly less than happy with the amenity perched on the hillside, notwithstanding the stained-glass window.

When a team of workmen started digging a vast hole in the terrace alongside the cottage I thought Guy had decided to put in a freshwater swimming pool. But within a few days a barge appeared and with considerable difficulty a huge fibreglass septic tank was hauled up to the terrace to hang precariously from the branch of a tree, pending installation.

The physics of the project bothered me somewhat because the cottage was built slap on the ground and I wondered how a satisfactory fall would be achieved from the bathroom into the tank.

This was never put to the test. It began to rain. It rained and it rained and it rained until there *was* a swimming pool on the terrace. At least there was until the sides of the excavation fell in and the adjacent path and steps collapsed.

I thought the last straw for Guy might have been when a council inspector came along and said, 'You can't do that there 'ere, mate.' But no. He cheerfully filled in the unwanted swimming pool, rebuilt the path and steps, and tackled the project another way. Soon, the loo with the stained-glass window was no more, a victim of modern plumbing.

Guy's companion as he weaved his way through minor disasters was a superb black Alsation. He bought Brett as a pup and the youngster idolised both Guy and Rummy. When Guy wasn't around, he followed Rummy everywhere, including the shortcut through my house, in one door and out the other.

In his own way, Brett had an even better life than his master. He played *all* the time. When he tired of lolloping with Rummy on the sandflat or making expeditions around the district he would return to the cottage, which invariably was left with doors wide open, and stretch out on Guy's bed.

It was a water bed.

One day, lying there, perhaps a little bored, as young dogs

will he gnawed the nearest thing to hand. This happened to be a corner of the water bed.

Now a king-size water bed holds nearly a thousand litres of water. . .

22

Sing if you must, Nellie Melba

Soft dragging sounds in the night. I snapped awake, listening intently. My right hand reached for the the ever-ready donger beside my bed.

What was it? Had I dreamt it? Where was the sound coming from?

Another sound, of creaking timber. It's nothing, I chided myself. Old wooden houses make strange noises: timber shrinks and expands with heat and cold, dryness and moisture.

But what I had heard was not a creaking-timber sort of sound.

It came again, a soft dragging sound like. . .like material such as the long, heavy train of a dress worn by a prima donna being dragged across a stage.

Trying to pin it down, my mind somehow ferreted out the story about Dame Nellie Melba that Jock and Jean had told me a few weeks before. I felt the skin tighten on my face and across the back of my scalp.

Nonsense! You don't believe in that sort of thing.

Again a soft dragging sound. . .

Nellie, oh Nellie, can it really be you appearing for yet another final performance? Sing if you must. In fact, I'd give anything to hear you sing, but please don't, if you don't mind, go shuffling around what is now my house scaring the bejesus out of me. I'm an innocent bystander. I wasn't even at the party when someone spilt a drink down your new dress or said you couldn't act or that you sang flat or whatever it was that gave you the huff causing you to come shuffling back here three-quarters of a century down the track.

A sudden, familiar rush of footsteps, caloomp, caloomp, caloomp. . .

It wasn't Nellie Melba dragging her train.

Oh my god, the possums have found a way into the bedroom side of the house! 'Edgar or Miss Clippy or whoever it is,' I said loudly to the ceiling, 'piss off! You're not welcome.'

I dropped the donger back on the carpet and lay there for some time listening first to the construction of a section of the Great Wall of China in the ceiling cavity above the hall which ran parallel with the living room, then a game of ten-pin bowling in one of the tunnels formed by the long, deep joists supporting the skillion roof and the ceiling above the bed-rooms and my office. It was apparent that the builders had left a stack of off-cut pieces of timber and other material lying around. I wondered what toy the possum had been playing with to create the dragging sound.

At last there was silence and I visualised the creature, all fluffy and furry, curled up as snug as could be, tail wrapped around its pink nose, snoring gently.

I, on the other hand, was as alert as Wellington before Waterloo.

After a while I started rummaging through my basket of sleeping tricks, murmuring in my head, 'I am relaxed. . . r-e-l-a-x-e-d. . .Sleep. . .S-l-e-e-p. . .*Curses on your fox-like head, Edgar, or whoever you are*. . .

I tried deep breathing, intoned a couple of yoga Ommmmmmms, sent a lotus blossom floating down the Ganges, tuned in to a dreamy bit of *The Pastoral Symphony*, then switched to the *La Boheme* aria 'They Call Me Mimi' which was disastrous, because I was back with Nellie Melba and could hear Jock's voice as he recounted his story.

Now my friend Jock was a man of contradictions. He loved talking to a subject and would improvise outrageously to win his point. But essentially he was a truthful person and if he told me that he had experienced something I would accept his story implicitly. He was an artist and had a strong inventive streak but he saw things clearly in black and white.

Jean was that sort of upper-middle-class English woman who simply did not brook nonsense.

As Jock told it, one evening the two were at home together reading and listening to music on their record player. In their library they had a number of very old recordings including several of Melba's. They enjoyed playing them occasionally, all the more because of Melba's association with the house. This particular evening they played just the one record, 'They Call Me Mimi', then by mutual consent agreed that they had had sufficient music for one night and concentrated on their reading.

Several years passed, then under somewhat similar circumstances they again played the 'Mimi' aria.

The record ended and both sat for a while without speaking. Jock lit a cigarette, then said in his deliberate way, 'Very strange. You know, Jean, while the record was playing I experienced an unusual sense of presence. I would swear someone else was in the room with us. Further, I sensed an odd. . .I can only describe it as the classic rushing of wind as though someone had opened the door on a stormy night.' He paused, then added, 'I didn't say anything at the time, but I experienced exactly the same sensations when we last played that record.'

And Jean replied quietly, 'So did I.'

My lecturer friend Robert was intrigued by Jock's story and on a number of occasions urged me to borrow the record to try to create a repeat performance. He's the sort of bloke who relishes dressing up for those 'Solve the Murder' games. Each time I replied stiffly that I wasn't interested in that sort of thing; besides, I like my house the way it is, thank you very much, and there are quite enough creatures clomping around uninvited in the middle of the night.

And clomp Edgar or whoever it was did. The next night I lay through a performance of the Seven Dwarfs' *Bavarian*

Schlossdanz fur Possum mit Lederhosen, a session of touch foot-ball, the construction of another section of the Great Wall of China and a game of postman's knock. Once I had accepted that I was wide awake I crawled out of bed and began thumbing through my ever-growing pile of reference books.

Within five minutes I put down the book I had been reading, sighed, and looked up at the ceiling. So it was pointless murdering the present occupant or even trapping it and banishing it to outer suburbia. The damage was already done. It, and who knows how many before, had laid a trail that was signposted for every possum to read: 'This way for commodious, free accommodation'. The removal of the present occupant would simply add the words, 'Vacant possession'.

The trail, it seemed, was laid by a scent that possums exude from glands under the chin, on the chest and near the anus. The scent trail is multipurpose: it enables a possum to retrace its steps and find its way out of tight situations, it defines territory—and it shows the way for other possums unto the umpteenth generation.

What's more, it was argued, trapping should only be used as a last resort because of the brushtail's obsession with territory. When a trapped possum is released in another area it may well have to battle for its slice of new territory. There was a chance it might not even survive.

The only thing to do, I decided, was find the possum's point of entry and block it off.

At dusk the following day, I settled into a comfortable chair in my bedroom with the previous weekend's still-unread newspapers, a stiff gin and tonic, and a large bowl of crisps. It could be a long wait before the possum chose to leave its lodgings.

I had finished the crisps, was considering the wisdom of a third gin and tonic, and had nearly demolished the weekend-ers when I heard sounds of movement above me. I put down the business section of the paper and stood, prepared to track my quarry.

Footsteps passed overhead, then a scrabbling sound came

from the living-room wall. 'So,' I muttered, 'it's climbing up the cavity between the walls.' There was a clatter under the house: the possum had jumped on to a stack of timber hoarded by Jock for some purpose still undefined. In a minute or two there was rustling in one of the camphor laurel trees.

There was little I could do at that hour. The possum returned in the early morning, belted a few balls along the ceiling in a chukka of polo, and settled down.

Later in the day, I climbed up through the trapdoor that Jock had made at the end of the hallway above the door for easy access to the ceiling and a platform he had built for storage. I suppose it could be called a loft. The trapdoor actually was a hinged section of the ceiling that extended the full width of the hallway.

I rolled out a strip of wire netting along the wall cavity between the living room and the hall, nailed it in place on one side only and folded it back. After the possum had left the ceiling that night I again went up through the trapdoor with a leadlight and nailed the netting over the cavity.

The assault on the wire some hours later was comparable with a massive German attack on the Western Front in 1915. The line held; the enemy was repulsed. But the signs were clear that both sides were settling in for a long period of warfare.

I clambered up through the trapdoor and by the light of a torch crawled along the planks that had been laid haphazardly on the joists above the hall ceiling, peering down the wall cavities on the office and bedroom side. I hadn't covered these with wire mesh the year before because I believed they were all blocked at the bottom.

Not a sign of life. Where were they? How *were* they now getting in?

Baffled, I returned to my desk.

Then pounding feet and scrabbling as a possum dived down a wall cavity with another possum in hot pursuit. Both hit the bottom. Gutteral coughs and fierce hisses. Back up the wall. . .along the ceiling above the hall. . .through a tunnel above my office. . .back again. . .down the wall. . .up the wall. . .along the hall. . .

The chase continued with ferocious coughs and hisses, down, up, across, as I thumped the wall and bellowed that this was *my* territory not their's, and they could buzz off and make love in the treetops—if you could call what they were on about love—or find a hollow tree to fight over the way God intended them to.

They didn't listen. Right, I said, it's the trap then.

By the time I had lugged the trap and the ladder from under the house and clambered into the ceiling all was quiet.

I set the trap and was sitting with my legs dangling over the edge of the platform about to step on to the ladder when I heard pounding to my right and a possum shot out from a tunnel above the back bedroom with another possum galloping close behind.

Too late! The lead possum didn't know the trapdoor was open.

It hurtled into space above the hall and the following happened in one impossible, miraculous instant. The possum saw me, looked down, a forepaw flashed back, grabbed the top of the wall and it flipped around in a 180-degree turn and went head-first down the wall cavity. Until that moment, I had always viewed the chase scenes in Tom and Jerry cartoons with a degree of scepticism. I recognised the disappearing tail end. It was a female possum I had named Stumpy. Her tail was only half the usual length; I don't know whether she was deformed or had met with an accident.

With equally lightning response her would-be lover dived after her and as soon as the two hit bottom there was a spate of fierce coughs and hisses. Silence.

'I ought to pour boiling oil over you,' I shouted down the cavity.

Then a clatter under the house. So this was where they were getting in. Here, at the back—or was it the front—of the house where it was close to the ground.

More wire mesh.

My series of defeats had made me wary of the scientific contention that because marsupials have smaller brains than placental mammals they were often outwitted when in competition.

Self-doubt can be corrosive; I, a mammal, had been outwitted by marsupials again and again. Come to think of it, I hadn't even won a contest with a duck.

I caught the male and reluctantly banished it to distant bushland.

I put the butt of the screwdriver to my ear and pressed the tip of the blade against the wall. No, nothing there. I moved further along the hall and again pressed the screwdriver blade against the wall. Nothing there. I tried several other places, unsuccessfully.

I was in the corner of the hall near the front door when I heard footsteps on the verandah and Don Wilcox looked in at me through the glass panel in the upper part of the door.

'Why are you walking around with a screwdriver in your ear?' he said.

'I'm possum hunting,' I said, opening the door.

'With a screwdriver in your ear?'

'It's a bush mechanic's stethoscope. Put the blade on a generator or electric motor and you can locate the scream of a worn bearing.'

'What's that got to do with possums?'

'I've managed to lock them out of the ceiling—for the moment, that is. Now there's one scratching in the wall cavity somewhere. I'm trying to track it down.'

'If you do,' said the Squire, 'and it's the one with a chopped-off tail, let me know. I want to strangle it with my own hands.'

'That's Stumpy. I think she's the one in here.' I tapped the wall. 'What's she done?'

'What does she *do*? Every night she waits until I'm just about asleep then leaps from the tree in front of our bedroom on to the verandah railing?'

'And that disturbs you?'

'Disturbs? The railing's wrought iron and it goes *doi-oi-oi-oi-ing* like the Town Hall clock. Scares the daylights out of me.'

'Fair enough,' I said. 'You have first option with the garrotte. Now, is this merely a social call or can I help you in some way?'

'The latter,' said Don. He indicated the screwdriver. 'You're a pretty technical bloke; can you help me to straighten a tree?'

'You're not jacking it up?' Remembering the time the Squire levelled the entire back section of his house.

He laughed. 'No. I'm just going to pull it straight. It's that young flowering gum I planted near the boundary.'

'It's leaning to get to the light,' I said. 'It's overshadowed by other trees. You can't win.'

'Oh yes I can. It can jolly well unlean. A tree's job is to grow *up*, not out.' Don yet again demonstrating his insistence on the vertical and the horizontal. An ex-British army officer, when he commanded, 'Attention!', even inanimate objects were expected to spring to attention.

The Squire's constant battle with plant life outclassed by far my skirmishes with possums. It was to the death. If a plant, tree or shrub didn't perform to his expectations, out it came.

So I helped give the young flowering gum a reprieve.

After we had hauled it straight with block and tackle and hogtied it to the foundations of his house, I resumed prowling the front hall with my ear to the butt of the screwdriver.

The Great Possum War it seemed was never ending. Like many a general in the field I was beaten again and again by the superior local knowledge of the enemy. I was a Johnny-come-lately, but the possums had been residents for generations. They knew every hidey hole, every conceivable point of entry to walls, to ceilings. Collectively, they knew more about the structure of the house than anyone apart from the architect, if there were one, and the builder.

My tussles with Stumpy had been going on for some time,

but I had never trapped her. Every now and then I would find her curled up asleep somewhere under the house.

Once, while searching for a piece of timber on a platform of potentially useful off-cuts Jock had somehow suspended just below floor level, I saw a possum sound asleep only a metre away. It stirred and raised its head. It was Stumpy.

We considered each other for perhaps a minute or so, then she gradually turned her head away and as though in slow motion uncurled herself and a baby clambered on to her back. She rose on all fours and moved so deliberately that she gave the impression she wasn't moving at all until she reached the beam below the wall cavities that I had blocked with wire netting long before, and eased her head inside until she was standing upright on the bearer.

I expected her to then shoot up the wall, but she continued to stand on the bearer, motionless, the baby clinging to her back. The cavity covered only her head and chest. She wasn't playing possum; she was playing ostrich. She couldn't see me, so I couldn't see her.

I left her standing there with her head in the wall and went upstairs to peel the spuds.

The solution was so obvious it was ridiculous. Instead of thrashing around in an unwinnable war I would extend the olive branch. I would provide the possums with alternative housing. I would use Jock's store of wood to build two, no three, possum boxes.

Any possum about to climb up a cavity wall in the hope of finding its way into a ceiling couldn't fail, it seemed to me, to be delighted by the discovery of a comfortable empty room just before commencing the scramble.

I nailed the boxes to bearers under the house at three points adjacent to what I believed to be well-established scent trails.

You might now, I said, addressing unseen possums, consider this establishment as your baronial manor. You have the north wing, the east wing and the west wing. Okay, so you're down instead of up; you've not got the penthouse. Remember beggers can't be choosers.

By way of welcome, I placed slices of apple at the openings of the boxes in much the way the management of a five-star hotel puts extravagant bowls of fruit in the rooms of valued guests.

Day after day, freshly placed apple remained untouched; the boxes remained empty. For the possums, it was the penthouse or nothing.

23

The ultimate question

The cicada walked at a deliberate pace along the branch of the jacaranda tree, then for no apparent reason put its six legs into reverse and walked backwards along the branch at precisely the same speed.

On an adjoining branch another cicada was doing the same thing, going forward, backwards. . .forward, backwards. . .

Why? Cicadas feed off the sap of plants and it would be reasonable to assume that they would explore and probe for the juiciest spot. But so far as I could see there was no pause, no probing. The cicadas simply walked forward then backwards, forward then backwards.

I wondered if Jock had ever observed this. He probably had. It was the sort of quirky behaviour that would have caught his observant eye. But he had never mentioned it on the many occasions when we had sat on the verandah to the right of my office when it was his verandah, his and Jean's, sipping a sundowner and watching the dollar birds wheeling in the late-afternoon summer sky catching a feast of cicadas on the wing.

I remembered his explanation of how the male cicada made its remarkable, insistent, ear-numbing drone, the muscles in sound-producing organs on either side of the base of the abdomen rapidly changing or crackling a rigid plate called a

tymbal. This crackling, said Jock, was amplified by membranes and an air chamber that almost fills the abdomen.

'Jock,' I wanted to say. 'What's your explanation as to why a cicada walks forward then backwards, forward then backwards? And I don't want you to make it up as you go.'

But I couldn't put the question to Jock. I had put my last question to my old friend.

Some months earlier, Jock had had a stroke while we were yarning in the dining area off my kitchen, the dining area that had been a stage where Nellie Melba had once sung.

He clung to life with the stubbornness I knew so well before his grip eased and he slipped away.

With his son, and with Jean's approval, I had scattered his ashes on the surface of the bay that afternoon the way he had once asked me to. He had finally gone to seek the answer to the ultimate question.

24

A new dimension

Soon after Rufus moved in with his beanbag, my friend Robert moved into the back bedroom.

Margot had accepted the acting editorship of the Far East English-language edition of her publication, which was a considerable pat on the back. By now, we were divorced and the move to Hong Kong was a considerable advancement in her career. To the puzzlement of many, our friendship survived and mutual respect remained. It seemed logical for her much-loved young ginger friend to join her much-loved tortoiseshell in company with the Richardson's silver-grey tabby. So I was now the non-owning chargehand of three cats.

Rufus had a distinctive personality and appearance. In many ways he was quite unlike a cat. A friend was convinced that he wasn't one at all; she said she was sure that if she ever got around to kissing him that he would turn into a handsome, red-headed prince.

I told her to go ahead; it was worth a try. But she never did. A pity.

So he grew to be a long, leggy cat with a smallish head and the gait and speed of a cheetah. Remarkably agile, he could make a standing leap of more than a metre straight up into the air and catch a moth with a clap of his forepaws. Margot swore that in sudden bursts of energy he would leap from the back of a sofa in the corner of the living room in her flat, hit the wall on the run, jump to the next wall and race along it to touch a third wall before jumping to the floor.

I've only seen this sort of thing done by daredevil fairground motorcyclists in an act billed 'Riding the Wall of Death'.

I can vouch for his speed from a standing, or rather lying, start. He was curled up sound asleep in his personal beanbag in the living room when Brett, now a full-grown dog, came through the back door taking a short cut down the hill. When level with Rufus he paused to give a sniff.

Rufus opened an eye to see Brett's great Alsatian head millimetres away. He unwound like a coiled spring, flipped out of the beanbag, and leapt for the verandah door.

It was closed.

Glass shattered as he hit the bottom panel like a bullet, the velocity carrying him through the door and down the steps.

I thought, my god, he's killed himself.

Brett turned and hurtled out the open back door with almost equal speed.

Rufus emerged from under the house ten minutes later. He had a small speck of blood on his nose, and the skin on the inside of the upper part of his right rear leg was neatly slit as if with a scalpel. The flesh was untouched. He didn't even seem dizzy.

But he wasn't an edgy, hyperactive cat. He just had to have something to do. Whereas Cumquat and Blossom would sit and watch while I was working in the garden, Rufus was forever investigating something, chasing lizards or anything that moved, rushing up trees to gaze down from a branch with a somewhat superior air.

Rufus was companionable; we became good pals. While he enjoyed company he was very much his own man, fiercely independent. It was difficult to pick him up at all let alone persuade him to settle in a lap. He enjoyed riding in the car, hindpaws on the edge of the seat, forepaws on the dashboard as he intently watched the traffic, and would accompany me on walks through the forest reserve at the head of the bay much as a dog would do.

Blossom and Cumquat barely tolerated him and he never lost his enjoyment in teasing them like a kid brother.

Sharing the house with myself and three cats had considerable attraction to Robert. He was lecturing at a nearby college, he appreciated the setting, and he saw the large central room as an ideal venue for fencing practice.

It was a good arrangement. We led independent lives, but as Robert lectured several nights a week he was often at home during the day and we would yarn whenever we emerged from our respective work areas. If he wasn't preparing his lectures or pursuing further study he was writing short stories. We found quite a lot to talk about.

When Jean Muir took a trip to England after Jock's death she asked a friend of a colleague of mine to mind her house. Said colleague and friend had previously minded my house when I was away on a trip to central Australia. By coincidence, Robert had known Tricia previously when they had been part of a young group sharing a house in trendy Paddington in the Eastern Suburbs. After Jean's return, we asked Tricia if she would care to join the household. She had become attached to the area; of course she would.

Tricia was a very special person who loved the world. A nurse, she was now specialising in occupational health. In between her work and pursuit of a lively social round, she somehow managed to find time to study subjects like anthropology just for fun. With her lightness of spirit, Tricia led something of a whirlwind existence; but when at home and the house was filled with mutual friends she presided as hostess extraordinaire.

The two added a new dimension to the old house which was built for good fellowship, not for a man to rattle around in on his own.

The fight was long and bloody as if each was driven by a hatred so intense that the only way it could be satisfied was to tear the other limb from limb.

Twenty-four hours before, the two had been romping happily together on the sandflat at low tide.

But all basic instincts aren't suffocated by suburbia. There can be only one top dog, and there comes a time when the young dog is not prepared to kowtow to the old dog any longer.

By now, Rummy was aging and although he was still extremely fit and strong he was tested to the limit by the superb black Alasation with the advantage of height, weight and youth. In the end, he was forced to back away.

Rummy and Brett never fought again, but their friendship was never restored. When they met on a path or on the road they would pass each other by as if they had never been formally introduced.

'It's for you,' Robert called.

'Hell!' I said, staring with disbelief at the blank screen of my new computer that told me that I had somehow contrived to lose every golden word I had written over the past hour and a half. 'Where is it?' I demanded of the box on the desk in front of me. 'Just where the hell is it?'

The box said nothing; my story failed to reappear.

'It's for you,' Robert repeated from the living room.

'And I haven't *saved!*' I shouted at the box. Pointlessly. So I addressed myself: 'Get into your thick head, man, that you have to save, save, save!'

'It's for you,' said Robert. 'It's Fiona.'

'Ohhh!' I snarled ungraciously. 'What does she want?'

'I really can't get the gist of it; something about watching a television screen.'

'Tell her I'm watching a blank computer screen. Can I ring her back?'

'I think you'd better speak to her. She sounds, well, kind of odd.'

'Ohhh. . .Okay.' Then contritely. 'Sorry, Robert, but I've just. . .'

'. . .lost the whole day's work,' said Robert. 'I can tell. You've got to keep saving, you know.'

'I know. I know. I know.' And picking up the phone extension on my desk said flatly, 'Fiona?'

Her voice sounded a little distant, vague. 'They've just gone,' she said. 'My guests—I had some old friends to afternoon tea—have just gone. But I feel I have to talk to someone. . .It's as though I've had one of those out-of-body experiences people talk about. I feel as though I'm outside my body looking at my own life as though it were being enacted on a television screen. . .'

And her voice drifted off.

A re-enactment, as they say in television news documentaries. . .

FIONA FISHER *in her living room serving afternoon tea to several ladies.* MARCUS, *aged ten and a half, rushes through a door opening to the garden.*

MARCUS (words tumbling out): Mummy, come quick! Tom's hung James in the boatshed.

[LADIES *show consternation.*]

FIONA [*calmly pouring tea*]: Yes, dear. I've been expecting it for some time.

MARCUS: I mean it, Mummy. I've saw it. Tom's hung James.

FIONA: Seen, darling. I've *seen* it. And the correct word is hanged. People are *hanged*; your schoolbag is *hung* on a peg. [*To one of the LADIES*] Milk and sugar, Helen?

MARCUS: Yes, Mummy. [*Grabbing her arm*] But come quick. Tom's hunged James.

FIONA: Marcus, you've already told me. In the boatshed. And the correct word is *hanged*. Just get that right; we'll deal with the adverb another time. Now do go outside and play.

MARCUS [*tugging at her arm*]: Truly, Mummy. You've got to come quick.

FIONA [*to the LADIES*]: Tom does get up to tricks. Remember how, as a toddler he thought he could fly, and in the end we had to put his cot mattress on the floor? Do excuse me for a moment. I had better check on what the boys are doing.

[*Boatshed interior. The sun streams brightly through the open, wide front door backlighting the figure of* JAMES *hanging from a rafter, a noose around his neck. The inert figure with wide-open, staring eyes, turns slowly, eerily. His brother,* TOM, *is leaning with a look of self-satisfaction against the door.*]

MARCUS [*from behind* FIONA, *triumphantly*]: I told you, Mummy. See! Tom's hunged James.

FIONA: Oh, my god! [*She rushes forward*] Tom, you idiot! Get the ladder! Quickly! [*Wraps her arms around her son's legs, pushes up against his weight.*]

JAMES [*looking down at* FIONA, *grinning*]: Hi, Mum! [*He pulls up his sweater. Another supporting rope can be seen looped around his chest and under his arms, leading up through the back of the sweater's neck to the rafter.*]

About a fortnight later Fiona rang again. 'Revenge is mine!' she declaimed.

'Huh?' I said.

James and Marcus, it transpired, had been instructed to have their shower in the downstairs bathroom which was at ground level.

Then James called, 'Mum, there's a snake in the bathroom.'

'Get into the shower,' said Fiona.

'But Mummy,' called Marcus, 'there *is* a snake in the shower.'

'If you expect me to believe that. . .' said Fiona. 'Get— into—the—shower!'

'But Mum,' James protested, 'we can't get in the shower with a snake.'

At which stage Fiona stormed down the steps to effect discipline. And through the open bathroom door she saw—a red-bellied black in the shower recess.

25

The cuckoo that got canned

I think I was thinking that I was dreaming when I heard it again and sat bolt upright in bed. It continued up the scale, *Whi, whi, whi, whi.* . . until it ran out of notes, then it started all over again from the bottom.

Oh, no! I groaned. Not in the camphor laurel trees. It can't be!

Whi, whi, whi, whi, whi. . .

A thump from the adjoining bedroom, clearly Robert sitting bolt upright in bed. 'What the hell's that?' he called.

'It's a brainfever bird,' I groaned.

'Huh?' said Robert.

'A semitone bird, a scale bird, a harbinger of bloody spring bird they also call it would you believe?'

'Oh?' Then, 'You mean a pallid cuckoo's moved in?'

'Correct,' I said. And off it went again, whistling *Whi, whi, whi, whi, whi.* . ., each note ending with a rising inflection which led to the next note, up, up, up. . .a sound maddeningly going nowhere, ending only to start from the bottom again—and again and again.

'We've got to get rid of it,' I said, swinging my legs out of bed.

'Now?' said Robert. 'You're joking. It's two o'clock in the morning.'

'It's no joke. You know those things move in for the summer, and if it sets up house in the camphor laurel trees we'll all end up cuckoo.'

I struggled into my dressing-gown and slippers and padded out on to the verandah. Robert joined me, bleary eyed, decidedly tousled. I was tempted to tell him his beard needed combing, but he wouldn't have been amused. I knew he'd been working on an assignment until after midnight.

We stared up at the branches. The call began again. No question. The pallid cuckoo was high up in one of the two camphor laurel trees. The camphor laurel trees overhang my office.

It suddenly stopped whistling and I opened my mouth to shout at it. But the shout ended up as a sort of gurgled *Yrrr. . .rrr. . . rrr. . .* I'd had enough practice with Dora and Charlie, but I was still at a loss to know what to shout at a bird.

The pallid cuckoo started again and instinctively I roared, 'Gitbehind!' which is the standard countryman's rebuke of a misbehaving dog.

Perched up the tree the bird knew it wasn't a dog and just kept on whistling up the scale.

'I think violence is necessary,' Robert said practically.

'You're right,' I said. I scurried down the steps, grabbed a loose stone from a pile it pleased me to call the rockery, and hurled it up into the branches. The lower branches, that is. I'm a lousy thrower, particularly up.

Robert walked down and scrabbled around for just the right stones. His throws outclassed mine, but were equally ineffectual. He shook his head, muttered, 'I've got to get some sleep,' and mumbling something about putting his head under the pillow shuffled back upstairs to his room.

The bird was high up in the trees, out of sight and out of range. After three or four more abortive throws during which time the creature kept whistling its head off I was ready to dash out and borrow a shotgun.

From being someone indifferent to birds I concede I had by now become something of a bird lover. But I'm a dog lover, too. I loved Rummy and everyone else's dog. I simply didn't want one of my own. I was prepared to love someone else's pallid cuckoo—from across the bay a few hundred metres away. But a pallid cuckoo up *my* camphor laurel tree, plonk above *my* office, was a horse of a different colour, so to speak.

When I had the boat business on the Pittwater I let a cottage behind the boatshed to a pleasant retired gentleman with a passion for sailing. He had survived machinegun fire, bursting shrapnel, bayonet attacks, mustard gas and trench feet in the First World War to remain one of the calmest men I've ever met. But every spring, within hours of the arrival of the first migrant pallid cuckoo he was near to being a quivering wreck.

Heavings and mutterings from Robert's room; not a squeak from Tricia's. It would have taken an invasion of vultures to disturb her.

I pulled the blankets over my head, buried my right ear in the pillow, and resolved to go to sleep. From several doors away I could hear the soft *croak, croak, croak* of the frogs that inhabited a fish pond on the Dennises' land. Excellent! I like frogs and find their calls soothing at any hour. If I had to hear something in the night I'd take frogs. *Croak, croak, croak* went Dennises' frogs. Beautiful! I lay there visualising the common eastern froglet, its big eyes bulging, its throat pulsing rhythmically to the beat of its call. Very soothing.

Then suddenly, *Whi, whi, whi, whi, whi* in frantic crescendo.

No! Reject it!

It was a test of willpower. All I would allow my ears to hear was *croak, croak, croak*. I would lock in on *croak, croak. croak.*

Yeah?

Whi, whi, whi.

No!

Croak, croak, croak.

Whi, whi, whi, whi.

Croak, croak croak.

Whi, whi, whi, whi, whi.

A rock rattled on the galvanised-iron roof above me and I heard Guy's tenant who had succeeded me in the house next door—which also was under the overhanging branches of one of the camphor laurel trees—scream in the night, '*Shuddup!*'

A disgruntled rumbling sound came from Robert's room. I half expected him to leap out of bed, whip the knob off the tip of his fencing foil, clamber up the camphor laurel and run the cuckoo through.

Lying there, telling myself I was asleep, I wondered what the creature was doing on this side of the bay. Every spring and summer a pallid cuckoo or two could be heard across the water just far enough away to be a source of wry amusement.

I wasn't amused now. I could see a long series of summer seasons ahead being driven out of my mind in what is as close to a Utopian setting as any human being has a right to expect in a late twentieth-century western city.

'That bloody bird,' Robert groaned at breakfast.

'What bird?' Tricia said brightly.

And the two went off to work.

Midmorning, my friend Barry called in on his way back to his office after doing an interview in my area. I gladly left my desk where nothing much was happening anyway and we went into the kitchen where I made coffee.

'You're looking peaked,' he said heartily.

'I had a rather restless night.'

'That's no good. You've got to get your sleep.' Then from above us came *whi, whi, whi*. . . 'Good god!' he exclaimed, sloshing his coffee on the kitchen floor. 'An exam bird!'

'A what?'

But he was striding to the front window where he peered up into the foliage of the camphor laurel trees. 'No question. It's an exam bird. At least that's what we call it. One comes around every year just as my poor kids are studying for the end-of-year exams. It's a miracle they've got past fourth grade.'

'Then you're an expert on them. What do you do?'

'Do? The best thing I've been able to do is turn the experience into a lesson in moral fortitude. I tell the kids they have to sweat it out. If you can take the exam bird, I say to them, you can take anything life's likely to dish up in the future.'

'Does it bother you, hearing it all day?'

'Me? No, not really. Of course, I'm not like you: I have to go into the office.' He didn't sit down again for the pleasant chat I had been anticipating, but gulped his coffee and walked out on to the verandah. 'If you want to stay sane,' he said, 'you'd better get rid of it.' And off he went.

A minute or so later Rufus came up the front steps with a little noisy miner clutched in his jaws miaowing through a mouthful of feathers. He deposited the corpse on the carpet and again miaowed at me in expectation of fulsome praise for his hunting prowess.

'No!' I said loudly, 'No!' Knowing that it was a pointless exercise to try to impose on a cat the commandment 'Thou shalt not kill', and snatched up the body before he could disembowel it. 'Instead of murdering innocents why don't you do something useful? Go climb the camphor laurel and scare the daylights out of that manic whistler.'

He growled at me from the back of his throat accusing me of foully nicking his noisy miner and stalked across to his beanbag where he made a thing of settling in and glared at me across the room.

I was giving the noisy miner a fitting burial in a corner of the garden when I remembered that the previous year a monstrous young pallid cuckoo had been brought to our side of the bay by its harassed foster mother, a yellow honeyeater a third of its size. The desperate little mother had discovered the tray of food that Jean Muir attached to the verandah railing, primarily for visiting rainbow lorikeets, and for her it must have seemed that all her worries were over. The baby cuckoo squatted on the edge of the tray, all fluffed out, squawking its head off while the honeyeater thrust food into its gaping beak with the relentless efficiency of a mechanical shovel.

Was this the same pallid cuckoo? Had it returned to the scene of its hatching—and a proven food supply? Didn't all migratory birds do this? Billions of 'em the world over.

Then for some reason my mind flicked back to a Tarzan movie I saw in my early teens in which an old bull elephant battled with evil ivory traders to return to its place of birth. Or was it to get to the graveyard of all elephants? My memory was confused—by the plot, and by the logic of a relationship between a pallid cuckoo and an elephant. And I recalled that I got confused by a number of things that Saturday afternoon, including the topography of the gorgeous Shirley Chambers whom I had at last persuaded to join me in an illicit liaison in the back row of the stalls when her mother thought she was doing her weekend homework with her friend Myra.

Question: How to get rid of a pallid cuckoo?

More from force of habit than the belief that I would find an answer I went to my bookshelves in search of an authoritative source and selected the *Complete Book of Australian Birds*. The index led me to ORDER CUCULIFORMES cuckoos FAMILY CUCULIDAE cuckoos, koels and coucals—and specifically, *Cuculus pallidus*.

I skipped down the page: 'At least 80 other species of birds play unwitting host to the egg and young of the pallid cuckoo. . .As with other cuckoos, the nestling pallid cuckoo ensures its survival by ejecting the eggs or young of its adoptive parents from the nest. . .Hairy caterpillars, grasshoppers and beetles make up the diet of the pallid cuckoo, and the hairs from the caterpillars line its stomach like fur. . .'

Really? I had a flash image of the inside of a bird looking like the outside of a caterpillar. Not a pretty sight.

'Voice: Loud melancholy whistling notes rising up the scale. Female has harsh single call. Male often calls at night. . .'

So it was a male up my camphor laurel trees. But what was the racket all about? Was he whistling simply for the hell of it? Was he, god forbid, establishing territory? Was his whistle a mating call?

At this last speculative thought I softened momentarily: I have known what it's like to whistle vainly in the night for a bird.

But what if he was successful? What if he was a hotshot cuckoo oozing sex appeal? Was I going to end up with a bevy of pallid cuckoo beauties perched all over the branches of my camphor laurels while this macho lug went up the scale and up the scale and up the scale?

I went out on to the verandah and listened for the responding 'harsh single call' which it stuck in my mind I had heard in years past.

There was none.

He didn't hear one either, and promptly started up the scale again.

Now stop and think, I told myself. In fact, think like a cuckoo; you should find that easier than trying to think like a duck. Maybe *he* goes to *her*. After all, he's been whistling frantically for twelve hours. At the first hint of a harsh single call he'll surely hurtle across the bay mad with desire.

It will be clear that at the root of my thinking was the fixation that all pallid cuckoos in this particular neck of the woods rightfully belonged on the other side of the bay. A mental block, maybe, but I believe an understandable one. Somehow, I had to convince the bird in my trees that his only hope of sexual fulfilment lay across the water.

My best chance of this, I decided, was female impersonation. Even though I'm not much of a whistler I believed I could handle a female pallid cuckoo.

I walked around the shoreline, stepping carefully over the oyster-covered rocks, until I was in the area which I had always thought of as pallid cuckoo territory. Looking fixedly across the bay at my camphor laurel trees I pursed my lips and let go with my version of a female pallid cuckoo's harsh single call. Not bad, I thought.

Silence from across the bay.

I tried again on a slightly higher note.

Still silence.

It's not good enough, I told myself. You've got to get right inside a pallid cuckoo; you've got to *be* a pallid cuckoo.

I closed my eyes for a spot of self-hypnosis, then tried again. After a few variations I felt I was getting the hang of it. Then. . .from across the bay an answering call, *whi, whi, whi, whi* faltering, then petering out on what would be *so* on the tonic solfa scale.

Encouraged, I gave another harsh single call.

Again, the responding rising notes, but even less certain, and this time trailing away at *me*.

The bird obviously was perplexed. Perhaps it detected a male timbre in my whistle, suspected a camp cuckoo, and wasn't falling for it. When a bloke sings his heart out the way this one was he's clearly intent on the real thing.

I tried a few more times, then got perplexed myself, reversed roles, and started whistling up the scale like Julie Andrews warbling for 'a deer, a female deer' on an alpine slope.

Still firmly ensconsed in my camphor laurel trees, the thing continued calling as I stumbled around the shoreline. By the time I reached my verandah I was nearly as bad a case as my First World War veteran tenant. '*Shuddup!*' I bellowed, echoing my neighbour of the night before, and picking up a metal drinks·tray which is usually lying on an occasional table, belted it as if it were a cymbal.

The cuckoo propped mid-note.

Ah ah!

Half a minute passed before it started again. Promptly, I bashed the tray. Once more it propped.

So! I had the answer. Yet again, man was about to triumph over nature.

I went under the house to the slab of timber I call my workbench but which, if I were honest, I should admit is my dumpbench, and foraged out an empty five-litre can I used for turpentine before it sprang a leak. I unscrewed the cap, found a largish steel bolt and tied it to the handle so that it dangled inside the can. I then tied a length of rope to the handle, and another length around the can so that it hung underneath it.

Dragging the lot behind me, I went to the camphor laurel tree nearest the house and, looping the end of the piece of rope tied to the can handle around my waist, climbed as high as I could without risking a broken leg. I threw the rope over a branch above me, again tied the end around my waist, and climbed down.

From the ground, I hauled on the rope until the can reached the branch high up in the tree, then made the rope fast.

I tossed the rope hanging from the bottom of the can through the open window of my office.

Then I went back to my desk. The end of the rope was within easy reach.

I was busily tapping the computer keyboard when the cuckoo started again. Swivelling my chair, I grabbed the rope, took up the slack and waited like an angler alert for a strike. The cuckoo was in full voice on the way to *la, tee, do* when I tugged the rope and shook it vigorously.

Clang, clang, clang went the bolt in the can up the tree. The *la* sort of choked in the cuckoo's throat.

It must have thought about this for a while before it started again. This time I rattled the can immediately.

It stopped. As the can was only a few metres under its tail I assume it was pondering on the connection.

The intervals between attempts at whistling grew longer. Each time, at the very first peep, I yanked on the rope. Each time, the cuckoo stopped dead. By now, it conceivably was experiencing emotions similar to those of a La Scala tenor being booed by the highly critical local audience before getting through bar one of 'Your tiny hand is frozen. . .'

Within half an hour it flew off.

Throughout the afternoon the cuckoo returned to the camphor laurel trees four more times. But at the first note, now scarcely raising my head from my work, my hand reached for the rope and—*clang, clang, clang*.

That night, faintly carried by the wind I heard *whi, whi, whi*. . . coming from across the bay. Lying in bed, I smiled contentedly. Then an anguished male cry, muted by distance, *Shuddup!*

I yawned and rolled over. There was no need to pull the blankets over my head.

26

The cocky and the kakapo

When it goes on and on and on, a cockatoo's usually engaging screech has all the charm of a chain saw.

Several times I left my desk and walked on to the verandah to locate the bird, scanning the sky to the west for a solitary cocky announcing to relatives in the Big Smoke that a country cousin had just blown in from the bush. But the sky was empty.

Finally, I concluded that the cockatoo was under the house next door. Guy Irving had recently sold the property and I hadn't yet met the new owners who were living in the top house. It was apparent that they had a cocky in a cage. The screeching continued for several hours.

The next day there was a repeat performance. And the next and the next, sometimes in the morning sometimes in the afternoon, it would seem, whenever the young wife went out.

You've got to switch off, I chided myself. You mightn't like birds being locked up in cages but that's the way things are. Anyway, the noise is muffled by being under the house and it's far enough away to be endured. Get on with the job.

I was lost in a story, fingers flying over the keys of my partially mastered computer on one of those rare occasions when words pour with the smoothness of water flowing over the spillway of a dam, when suddenly, close by, the cockatoo's screeching hit with the impact of a rock band.

My head swivelled to the left. A large sulphur-crested cockatoo was flattened against the wires of a cage standing on the stone flagging in the courtyard next door. Its yellow-tinged wings were extended as far as they could go in the confined space, its yellow crest was erect and angry, and it was screeching blue murder.

The spillway of inspiration suddenly dried up.

I was watching the cockatoo trying to wrench off a wire with its beak when I heard Robert come in the back door and walk through to my office. 'Where has *that* come from?' he said over my shoulder.

'The new people have kept it under the house until now,' I said. 'It's been performing every day while you've been at work. Do you have a spare office I could move into at the college?'

'You could apply on compassionate grounds. Getting any work done?'

'I was on a dream trip when this started five minutes ago.'

'Oooh,' he said through pursed lips. He knows how hard this business is. 'What are you going to do?'

'A good question. I suppose I can introduce myself and by way of welcome to the district tell them their cockatoo is driving me bananas. Then they could say, Too bad, and incidentally we're not very happy about your three cats piddling in our garden.'

'Yes, they could say that.'

'Even though it's driving me bananas I'm more concerned for the cocky. The way it's carrying on I'd say it's an adult bird someone has trapped and slapped in that tit of a cage. It's stir crazy: it can't even spread its wings. It'll kill itself trying to get out, or at best wreck its vocal chords.'

'So what are you going to do?' Robert asked again.

At which I saw myself as a country kid in discussion with a couple of pals who had conceived a commercial project to trap zebra finches. Lured by the prospect of riches I agreed to show them where the birds could be found: they knew I spent half my spare time exploring the bush.

The trap was a wire cage with three compartments. A tame

bird was put in the central compartment and its calls attracted wild finches which, with the further inducement of bird seed, hopped into the adjacent traps.

My pals probably have never worked out why the project was such a dismal failure in a finch-rich area. Sentiment overcame avarice. Each time we were due to check the trap I would get there early and set the catch free.

Now, many years on, I brushed aside an evil thought.

But as day succeeded day the thought kept returning. Each time my new neighbours went out and put the cocky in the courtyard, presumably to enjoy the open air, work became almost impossible. The cockatoo screeched endlessly and thrashed frantically around its cage within twenty metres of my office window.

Robert and I earnestly discussed the situation. We were both convinced that the bird was an adult that had met the fate proposed for the zebra finches. If so, it was highly unlikely that the owners would agree to let it go. There seemed to be no alternative to subterfuge; if I spoke to them and they declined to act I would have declared my hand. When Rummy and one of his mates trotted by and went up to the cage to investigate the din they unwittingly presented me with the core of a plan. I made a reconnaisance.

The following day, after the cockatoo had been screeching for twenty minutes and the coast seemed clear, I crossed to the courtyard. As I approached, the bird quietened and looked at me with interest. I went straight to work.

The reconnaisance had revealed that the cage simply sat on a galvanised base with the locking clips undone. My intention was to give the impression that a dog had knocked over the cage. Slowly, so as not to frighten the bird, I laid the cage on its side exposing the open end. The cockatoo seemed to appreciate the new arrangement. It walked upside down along the wire and out the end and sat on top of the cage. Even when you hate it, it's not always easy to leave home.

The deed done, I returned to my office and from the side window observed the cockatoo walk across the courtyard and climb a low fence smothered in wisteria vine. Here, it proceeded to wreck havoc with the spring flush of pendulous purple blossoms. Not a screech. All very satisfactory I thought; it will soon fly off. And in blissful silence I sat down at my desk. When I looked up some time later the bird had gone.

Midafternoon I heard a woman's voice calling, 'Easty!Easty!'

I glanced through the side window. The cage had been replaced on its base.

As I punched words into the computer I could hear the woman calling urgently, '*Easty! Easty!*'

The voice went down the path to the waterfront then came back up the hill, crossed to the second terrace below my house and came up the path towards me. '*Easty! Easty!. . .Easty! Easty!*'

Uh uh. Guess I'll have to ride it out.

'Excuse me.'

I stood and looked down from the window at an attractive young woman with tears streaming down her face. 'Have you seen our cockatoo? He's got out. He doesn't know how to fend for himself. He can't fly.'

Can't fly? Oh hell! I thought. Don't tell me they've had it since it was an egg.

I'm a hopeless liar: if I were a member of MI5 I'd cop the firing squad on my first spying assignment. But I had to bluff it through. Feeling rotten with guilt I was now as anxious to locate the pedestrian cockatoo as my tear-stained neighbour whose name I learned was Laura Easton. I felt even lousier when I found her to be totally charming as she apologised profusely for the noise the cockatoo had been making. They had been given the bird several years before and while they regarded it with affection they were as stymied as I was to know what to do about the racket it made.

So I joined Laura in 'Easty! Easty-ing!' up and down the hillside. All to no point. Easty was either lying low enjoying his new-found freedom, or already had been gulped by Rummy or one of his pals.

I returned to my desk to wallow in guilt.

Just before dusk the Easty calls were renewed, this time as

a duet. Laura's husband, Geoff, was home from his office. The calls came from my lower terrace. I looked out of the window. The cockatoo was a splodge of white on a lower branch of one of the Norfolk Island pines.

Great! It was still alive. I thought it best to stay clear.

Every now and then Easty gave a screech of acknowledgement to the calls, raised his yellow crest, bobbed up and down and spread his wings as though about to take off. But he didn't. Instead he climbed up. And up. I was reminded of the New Zealand kakapo, a large flightless bird that perambulates along footpaths it has made and is now dangerously close to extinction.

Evolution had a hiccup with the kakapo. Having given up flight, it learned how to climb trees for food—or perhaps that came first. But it only learned how to climb up; it never learned how to climb down. I understand that when a kakapo has gone as far as it wishes to go up a tree it simply jumps. It crashes down through the branches, hits the ground with a thump, shakes itself, then plods along to the next tree no doubt with its head ringing.

The Easty calls continued into the early torch-lit evening. Scraps of sentences drifted up from the terrace: '. . .chilly. . . catch cold. . .cloth over his cage. . .'

With darkness, it was apparent that Easty had a tough night ahead; he was like a tenderfoot Boy Scout at his first camp.

The Easty calls resumed at daybreak. I padded through to my office. The cocky had somehow made its way down to the second lowest branch on the pine tree: Laura and Geoff were on the terrace shaking tins containing bird seed.

This could work. A proven method. My father used to tell the story of the only way he could catch the stallion he rode as a young man. He would rattle corn in an old enamel chamber pot and that sucker of a stallion would come racing from the far corner of the home paddock every time.

Cautiously, Easty began to climb down the trunk with the aid of his strong curved beak. Well, he had learned something.

Uh uh! Laura and Geoff were standing near the tip of the lowest branch. Instead of carrying on to the ground, Easty stepped on to the branch and walked towards them. When he reached the end he screeched, raised his crest, spread his wings and bobbed up and down. He was a timid small boy on the top springboard of a diving tower.

For a moment I considered trying to 'talk him down' the way they give radio instructions to a passenger in a light plane when the pilot has had a heart attack. But I knew the instructions wouldn't get through. I'd proved with Dora that I don't have a direct line to birds.

'Just jump.' I finally muttered. 'You don't have to know how to fly. Just spread your wings and jump.'

Nobody was getting anywhere when I remembered that I had seen a long timber batten under the house among Jock's treasures, a cover strip he had bought and never used.

I took it down and gave it to Geoff. It was just long enough to reach the branch near the cockatoo's claws.

Easty got the drift. He stepped on to the batten and gingerly edged down it crabwise until he reached Geoff's hand then walked confidently along his arm to perch on his shoulder.

Jock would have been delighted. He always knew that long length of batten would come in handy one day.

Metophorically speaking, there I was down on one knee, proposing to Tricia.

'Tricia,' I said with admirably controlled emotion, 'I am deeply and profoundly in love with you. I believe I have been since I first met you. . .Well, possibly the second time I met you, when you came to this house to find me hobbling around with an appalling blood blister on my left great toe having carelessly dropped a lump of steel on it just as I was about to leave for central Australia.

' "I don't want sympathy," I said through gritted teeth. "I just want to be able to climb Ayers Rock." '

'I remember your every word: "Would you get me a slide clip, a candle and a box of matches?" '

' "What's this?" I said. "Witchcraft?" '

'You merely raised an eyebrow, straightened the steel clip, lit the candle, and heated the tip of the clip until it glowed red. Then you bored a hole right through my left great toenail.

'Whereupon, the blood that had been compressed between flesh and nail—and the dreadful pain—flowed away.

'I should have taken you in my arms and said, "Never leave me!" '

'But I now know that you would have said wryly: "I once worked with a doctor, a happily married man, who too was spontaneously proposed to, in his case, by a large Irish plumber who had jammed his thumbnail in his stilson wrench." '

'So I didn't say, "Never leave me." I foolishly got in my four-wheel drive and headed for Alice Springs.

'This was a mistake. Since you have been here—with some acknowledgement to Robert's presence—the house has been filled with joy and laughter, witty, intelligent and highly amusing conversation, with splendid dinners and lunches on the verandah, on the terrace and in the rock-walled dining room, and with music, albeit sometimes at a distressingly amateur level.

'It's been one of the world's great friendships. But can't we make it more than that? We could have a wonderful life together. Will you marry me?'

Tricia heard me out. But she hadn't really heard me because I hadn't said all that at all.

What I actually said was, 'Err, mumble, err, mumble, err'. My track record in the marriage stakes did not imbue me with confidence. Nor, clearly, her.

She sat quietly for a while then said gently, 'I hope you'll understand. . .but I feel I already have a wonderful life. I'm very lucky. If I didn't have my life it's the sort of life I'd wish I did have. Does that make sense? I value your friendship and I've loved sharing your house. It's been fun.' She paused, then continued, 'By the way, there's something I want to tell you. I've found an apartment I'm thinking of buying overlooking the harbour near the bridge. I was rather hoping you'd come and look at it with me. I'd really appreciate your opinion.'

Which is the price one pays for loving a free spirit.

But then, *I* too was a free spirit.

This production was to have several, non-consecutive, repeat performances. None received a nomination for an Academy Award.

I glanced out of the side window. Easty was perched on one leg on the vine-covered courtyard fence nibbling at the last of the wisteria blossoms held delicately in the other claw.

He can't be! He is! He's out again!

My hand was reaching for the telephone when I stopped to reconsider. I had had several relatively quiet days of great value. When the Easton's learned that I was working at home they considerately said they would keep the birdcage under their house. This was great for me, but I knew that the Dennises on the other side were getting full blast Easty's protestations at being left alone. I had no alternative; I rang.

'Thanks for calling, but we've let him out,' said Laura. 'He's unhappy when he's left alone in his cage and we can't alienate the neighbours. We've decided to let him take his chances. The door of his cage is open and he's been walking in and out. With luck he'll learn to fly, but he'll know he can always come back.'

After half an hour or so, Easty began flapping his wings. With a startled expression he left the fence and was airborne for a few metres. He then walked home down the path.

Day by day, Easty's proficiency improved but he still had a lot to learn. I wished that somehow I could introduce him to Dora who also had taken up flying as a mature-age student: she would have been able to pass on a few tips. But Dora had not been with us for some time now. She must have been eleven or more before she winged her way to duck heaven. So, as things were, Easty was on his own.

The plan worked to everyone's satisfaction including Easty's. During the day, he would flap and stroll around the perimeter of the house returning to his cage whenever he was peckish or felt like a nap. At dusk, he put himself to bed and the cage was covered. Even though the door was open all the time he never attempted to leave the cage until the cover was removed.

All went well for a week, then one night Easty didn't return.

Once more, the cry *'Easty! Easty!'* rang around the bay but there was no responding screech or rush of wings.

By dusk the following day he still hadn't returned. Many birds that escape or are released after being bred in captivity do not survive. They are unaccustomed to exposure to the weather, are untrained to find their own food and they are easy game for predators such as cats and dogs. They are also vulnerable to attack from other birds which are ruthless when it comes to defending their territory against a lone intruder. Even though he was a big healthy bird Easty's chances didn't look good.

Early on the morning of the third day I had just started my walk when I saw a lone cockatoo perched on a low branch of a tree. It looked like Easty, but I wasn't familiar with any distinguishing marks or chracteristics.

'Hello boy,' I said. 'Are you Easty?'

The bird made no response. It looked at me rather glumly. But it had to be Easty. A wild cockatoo would be happily feeding at that hour, not sitting on a branch looking glum.

'Don't move,' I said. 'I'll be right back.' I hurried down to the Eastons' and knocked on the door. Laura answered. She was in her dressing-gown but she rushed straight up the path.

It was Easty all right. His crest shot up at the sight of Laura and he squawked a greeting. But his flying had clearly regressed. Perhaps he had had a prang and without an instructor to send him straight back up in the air again was funking it, as Biggles would have said.

I tried the jump routine again but his claws seemed glued to the branch. 'You stay with him,' I said to Laura. 'I'll get a ladder. He's within reach.'

Laura climbed up, held out her hand, and Easty stepped aboard.

I'd done this a number of times with cats, but this seemed

ridiculous. Any healthy, adult bird that has to be rescued with a ladder does not, to my mind, have a promising future.

But I was wrong. The Eastons stuck to their guns: Easty's cage door was left open and he was free to come and go. After a good breakfast, which probably settled his nerves as effectively as a slug of brandy, he took off on another solo training flight. Biggles would have been proud of him: he showed pluck.

From now on there was no turning back: Easty was on his way to being an ace. His take-offs were impeccable and his landings smooth whether from a branch or solid ground; he weaved his way through trees at full throttle, dodging trunks and branches as though computer controlled; he mastered cockatoo aerobatics, diving and climbing, swooping and wheeling. Increasingly, he was away all day, but in the late afternoon I would hear him screech and he would swoop past my window, the underside of his wings flashing yellow, to land on the Easton's front terrace. Then he would make his way under the house to his cage and birdseed supper.

It was great to see him flying free enjoying the best of both worlds, but as he was so friendly I was concerned that he might drop in somewhere to make a courtesy call and find himself back where he started—in a cage.

To make it clear that he was not a waif I had the local jeweller engrave his name and telephone number on a strip of aluminium and we banded him.

Then one night Laura rang: 'Easty hasn't come home. Have you seen him?'

'It's to be expected,' I said. 'He's probably spending the night out. He'll be back for his birdseed.'

But several days went by. The district was scoured. Not a sign of Easty. He was posted as 'Missing'.

Then the Eastons had a phone call from someone living a few blocks away: 'I think we have your cockatoo. He flew in and we put him in a cage to look after him. But we've just noticed the band with your telephone number.'

A likely story, 'just noticed the band'. They thought they had a cocky for free. Doubtless, Easty's attractions had faded

after a few days of listening to his protests at again being incarcerated.

This time Easty was rescued by car; at least he no longer needed a ladder.

And so the life of Riley became the life of Easty. Most nights he returned to his cage but quite often he was away for a day or two. The band proved to be very effective. The Eastons got more phone calls from people who plainly had adopted him and paid the price and from others who were genuinely concerned that he was lost. At first, Geoff or Laura dashed around immediately to collect him. Then they began to say, 'Thank you very much, we'll drop by in the morning'. Finally they reached the stage of saying, 'Thanks for calling, but just throw him out. He'll fly home when he's hungry'.

Then one morning I unfolded the local paper to see the headline: COCKY VANDAL IS A CASE FOR THE BEAK. And there on the front page was a picture of Easty perched on a clothes line nibbling a peg.

The story, implying rape and pillage, was about a vandal cockatoo that was raiding clothes lines in the district. Its technique was to pull off pegs one after the other until the entire load of washing had fallen to the ground. It would then disappear as mysteriously as it had arrived.

Alienation of immediate neighbours was one thing, alienation of an entire neighbourhood was another. The Eastons declared that Easty had to go. I found myself protesting; he couldn't be locked up again, not now.

Foraging through my mind for an answer to the problem, I remembered friends who had a sheep property near Bathurst to the west of Sydney. They were exceptional in that they belonged to the minority among people who raise stock for a living: they truly loved animals. I recalled they had built a large aviary near their house where they cared for birds they found in distress until they were well enough to be released again.

'Would we like a cockatoo?' they whooped over the phone. 'This is incredible luck! We've been trying to buy a cockatooo for months.'

The unavailability of caged cockies in country districts is not surprising. With millions of cockatoos swooping over fields of grain and orchards, farmers are more inclined to think of getting out the shotgun for mass murder rather than keeping just one as a pet.

I had another band made with his new telephone number engraved and Easty became a true country cocky. He readily adapted to life on a sheep station dividing his time between flying with flocks of wild cockatoos and helping out at the homestead. He still had more than a passing interest in clothes pegs and became remarkably efficient at unscrewing loose nuts on motorcycles and machinery with his beak.

On occasions when I see a lone cockatoo wheeling and screeching above the bay I wonder if. . .

But I'm sure that if it were Easty he'd drop in to say 'G'day'.

27

So now we know

At last I have the answer to my long-ago scribbled note, 'Spiny anteaters: just how do they do it?' Only recently I opened a copy of The Australian Museum Trust's excellent magazine *Australian Natural History*, or *ANH* as it's popularly known, and to my delight came across a fascinating article titled 'Overcoming a prickly problem'.

Environmental physiologist Dr Peggy Rismiller, at this time visiting research fellow at the Department of Anatomy and Histology, University of Adelaide, and biologist–wildlife photographer Mike McKelvey, had been working full time in the field on Kangaroo Island to the southwest of Adelaide, studying all aspects of the life of the spiny anteater or short-beaked echidna.

Without a blush, they have spied on the courtship procedures of *Tachyglossus aculeatus* and have revealed their innermost secrets. Is nothing sacred?

Naturally, now I can't keep *my* mouth shut.

They have confirmed the 'echidna trains' observed by fellow scientists over the years that must be among the more heart-rendering accounts of unrequited love.

Up to ten male spiny anteaters have been observed trundling along nose to tail in the wake of a female clearly with one common thought in mind. This must boost the girl's self-esteem no end. The tail-ender is often a precocious subadult without a chance in the world, it seems, just going along for the ride to learn a thing or two.

The chaps certainly get top marks for persistence. Who could fail to be impressed by him dubbed Casanova.

I quote: 'Casanova [was found] with Zoey on two consecutive days before his tracking signal suddenly disappeared. He showed up three days later two kilometres away, with Niki, and another ten days and a further two kilometres away he was found with Big Mama. During Casanova's six weeks of courting he lost 800 grams, nearly 25 per cent of his body mass.'

As C.J. Dennis would say: 'I dips me lid.'

Now to the nitty gritty.

'During mating,' says Dr Rismiller, 'the female lies flat on her stomach, often with her head and front legs partially dug in at the base of a shrub or small tree. The male or males begin digging along either side of the female. If more than two males are present, they push each other aside, digging not only along[side] the female, but also around the vegetation. At some point one of the males will turn to his opponent and begin a head-on-head pushing contest until only one remains in the dug-out trench around the female. This male continues to dig on one side of the female, stroking her spines and attempting to lift her tail end with one of his hind feet. He finally succeeds in raising her enough to be able to place his tail under hers while lying on his side. This 'foreplay' may take up to four hours.

'Once in position the male extends his penis. . .Coupling is completed after 30 to 180 minutes and the animals go their separate ways.'

To a well-earned rest, I'd say.

28

Prophesy fulfilled

Over the years I was growing up I never knew the lid of the piano in our house to be closed. Had my parents been aware that this was to be the situation they probably could have done a deal with the salesman and saved on the price of the lid. It was an unnecessary appendage to the instrument; it served no function other than that the little hinged platform screwed to the underside held the music.

Both my mother and sister played the piano, I played the fiddle to mother's accompaniment, all four members of the family sang. I guess it was a pretty noisy household. But we didn't bother the neighbours because they, too, were forever making music. We lived in that sort of town. At the drop of a hat the word would go around and that evening half the neighbourhood crowded into our living room to play their party pieces and sing their heads off.

Dad specialised in ballads that, to me as a boy, were either wonderfully exciting—or plain soppy. I would be enthralled as he sang in his fair baritone, 'Trumpeter what are you sounding now, is it the call I'm seeking?. . .', then swung into, 'A pirate king of the air am I, on pinions white I roam the sky. . .', and with little encouragement gave a second encore boasting, 'I am a bandellero, a king with the sward for pillow. . .'

All ripping stuff, and for years I remained impressed by the brigand who was so tough he slept with his head on his sword. I saw it with the sharp edge up. I was slow to learn that a *sward* is a patch of grass.

But I was both bored and embarrassed when he was in the mood for soppy songs. It just didn't seem right for a father who could ride a horse and drive a car better than anyone else in the whole world, and lift huge weights that I was sure no other kid's father could even get off the floor, to be singing 'Believe me if all those endearing young charms, which I gaze on so fondly today, were to change by tomorrow and flee in my arms, like fairy gifts fading away. . .' Then there was the one that started, 'At seventeen he fell in love quite madly with eyes of a tender blue. . .' and ground its way relentlessly through the poor man's amorous misadventures until it finally declaimed, 'And when he thought he was past love, it was then he met his last love, and he loved her as he'd never loved before'.

I wonder if my father would have kept this song in his repertoire had he guessed it was prophetic of the torturous path through life that his son was to take. He probably would have: it had a very happy ending.

Tricia and I were married on the terrace under the liquid amber. It was an event that met with the universal approval of family and friends who declared it should have happened years before. I agreed with this wholeheartedly, but when one free spirit meets another free spirit. . .

It was weird. Repeatedly, I would walk on to the verandah to see a pet's feeding bowl half-full of food in the middle of the terrace below the house pretty much on the spot where our wedding ceremony had taken place. Somehow it smacked of a votive offering.

Inquiries revealed that the bowls belonged to neighbours on either side. At first, I would personally return the bowls, but this became such a chore that I ended up flicking them in the appropriate direction like frisbies.

One morning, I looked out from my office to see Rummy walking across the lower terrace. Advancing years had changed his snappy step to a rolling gait, but even apart from that he looked different. For a moment I thought he had been initiated into the African tribe whose members wear what appears to be a pizza plate in the lower lip. Then I saw that he had a bowl clamped in his jaws.

I watched him making heavy weather climbing up the steps towards me, then as he reached the terrace I opened a window and said sharply, 'Rummy! What's with this rash of kleptomania?'

He scarcely broke his pace. He put the bowl down carefully on the lawn without spilling a drop, merely flicked an eye at me, and kept walking up the path and around the house.

Rummy had never been a greedy dog. It seemed that he was simply providing for his old age, putting a little aside every now and then near the house where he had grown up. He had become a hoarder.

As time went by, Rummy became increasingly frail and quite deaf. He was still a happy, laughing dog, but when his sight began to fail rapidly, Jean was concerned that he would walk off one of the terraces he used to leap in a couple of bounds and sustain a severe injury.

So the day came when Robert and I took him in the car on his last visit to the vet.

We buried him against the rock wall on the lower terrace which had been one of his favourite trails. He was nineteen. Not bad for a dingo with a price on its head.

Rummy was in good company with Cumquat and several of my friend Pat's beloved moggies. Blossom had long since returned to Richardson's land which was now incorporated in the bush reserve at the head of the bay. Eventually, the animals on the terrace were joined by Rufus. He had been my pal for seventeen years.

It was very clear where one possum was. It was the filling in a toasted sandwich layered between the ceiling and the skillion roof over the laundry. The temperature was around thirty degrees in the shade; I couldn't guess what it was in the hundred-millimetre gap under the sheets of galvanised iron being directly bombarded by the sun's rays.

The black brush of the possum's tail and one grey hind leg with a pink paw dangled limply from the gap at the outer edge of the ceiling seeking fresh air. Had I stood on tiptoe I could have reached up and given the tail a tug, but that would have been like assaulting the oldest resident in a boarding house for the genteel who have come upon hard times.

This particular possum had been a guest in the laundry ceiling for a number of years. It was welcome. The ceiling was made of a tough water-impervious material; the gap did not give access to the rest of the house. We were quite happy to share the laundry ceiling—the possum above, us below.

The bedroom ceiling—the west wing—was another matter. And whoever was presently up there was a master tactician who cunningly crept in heaven knows where, made bed, laid on it. No wild parties before hopping between the sheets, no Rugby games, no major construction work. Just persistent scratching, the elbow knocking the ceiling like a dogged bailiff at the front door—at three, four or five in the morning.

I was forced to set the trap.

But the wooden box and the lump of apple hooked to the 'trigger' inside were ignored, although the pieces of apple making a trail to the mouth of the trap were missing each morning.

On the fifth day I switched tactics. I placed only one small piece of apple outside the trap and another smaller piece just inside. This was carefully calculated to create an unquenched lust for apple. A large, fresh, juicy piece hung from the 'trigger'.

Just after dusk I heard the door of the trap fall shut and within five minutes there was a great rattling in the ceiling as the possum scratched furiously at the door then squirmed around to attack the door the other end.

After we had had dinner I climbed into the ceiling to retrieve the trap and drove to the patch of bush several kilometres away where I always released the possums I caught. Invariably, they had to be prodded out of the trap then they would race off and shoot up the nearest tree.

I lifted the door of the trap a little and saw a grey hump of possum fur. Wrong end. I lifted the other door and saw a pink nose in the light of the torch. I turned the trap so that the nose faced the bush and removed the door. Nothing happened. I removed the other door and gave a gentle prod with a stick.

A possum walked out and with as much dignity as the species is capable of mustering set off along the track. I recognised the all-too-familiar tail. 'Stumpy!' I called.

The old possum stopped, half-turned, and looked back at me.

'I didn't know it was you,' I said to her and the trees. And I thought of the years she had lived around, under and in the house above the harbour. She probably had been born there. I wondered how she would manage on rainy nights if she couldn't find a dry hollow in a tree, and if she could defend herself if she had to fight for territory.

Had she proposed it, I believe I would have been prepared to sit down and talk things through with her; a deep meaningful chat about territorial rights, division of property and that sort of thing. 'Stumpy,' I would have said, 'let's call it quits. You promise to keep out of my ceiling and I promise to keep out of your trees. You can even have permanent residence under the house. Cross my heart and spit. Now hop back in the trap and we'll go home.'

But she looked at me with an expression that I interpreted as more in sorrow than in anger, turned away, and walked into the bush.

The honking of a horn made me realise that I was driving too slowly along the two-lane road with little room for passing. I was thinking, and my foot had eased off the accelerator.

I speeded up but continued thinking about the now-empty trap in the back of the car and the accommodation problems

possums have in suburbia. I felt badly about old Stumpy; all she wanted was a snug spot to curl up in in daylight hours. When outside the house she wasn't any trouble at all. We didn't mind possums tromping over the roof; we didn't really mind the ruckus of love and war.

Unquestionably, the crux of the problem was a shortage of the right kind of tree, I mused. Before Europeans came on the scene to chop and burn and carve the land into little squares on which they built their wooden, brick and stone boxes, there were countless billions of the right kind of tree. They were predominantly eucalypts, predestined to have branches snap off in storms leaving jagged butts which eventually hollow at the tips; develop knobbly extrusions on their trunks which in time degenerate forming cracks and crevices; and either through bushfires, termites or sheer old age have their trunks scooped out to form nature's own high-rise apartments. Accommodation had never been a problem for birds and tree-climbing beasties.

Now look what's growing in front of me. True, they're beautiful trees—jacarandas, camphor laurels, a liquid amber, pine trees—but they're as foreign to this country as sauerkraut and schnitzel. No wonder Stumpy and his mates say, Come on, a fair thing is a fair thing; you took our trees to build your houses and plant your gardens, aren't we entitled to a corner of the ceiling.

And I thought about the possum boxes I had made to no avail several years before.

I now knew that the design had been wrong and that it had been pointless putting them under the house. Brushtails like to be at least four metres above the ground, a possum person at the zoo had told me, and they like a deep hollow to crawl down into. She had shown me the boxes they use at the zoo. The construction was quite simple.

Now, I thought, if I have, say, three boxes in the trees around the house the possums surely will use them rather than having to battle their way into the ceiling every night. Then I'll have three permanent residents who won't allow other possums to move in. This is quite rational: they are extremely territorial. It will be like having possum watchdogs. Yes, I know I'm busy and it's not just a five-minute job, but I'm always busy: being busy is all-too-often an excuse for not getting things done. It will probably take me a full day to make them—well, maybe a day and a bit. But it really will be a worthwhile investment in time.

Won't it?

Acknowledgements

I would like to thank members of the staff of The Australian Museum for their helpful advice and comments, especially Dr Michael Gray, curator in the Arachnology Department; Walter Boles, head of the Ornithology Department; and Linda Gibson, technical officer in the Mammals Department. I would also like to thank Bernice Walters, founder of the Australian Native Dog Training Society.

Among the many publications I have found both informative and fascinating to read are *The Australian Encyclopedia* published by The Australian Geographic Society; *The Australian Museum Complete Book of Australian Mammals*, Angus & Robertson; the *Reader's Digest Complete Book of Australian Birds*, The Reader's Digest; *A Very Elegant Animal the Dingo* by Roland Breckwoldt, published by Angus & Robertson; *A Field Guide to Australian Birds* by Peter Slater, published by Rigby; the *Australian Geographic* magazine published by The Australian Geographic Society; *Australian Natural History (ANH)*, the magazine of The Australian Museum Trust; and *Urban Wildlife of New South Wales*, edited by John Pastorelli and published by Angus & Robertson.